ADVANCE PRAISE FOR BURST

"In *Burst*, Kevin Wells shares how the Catholic prayers and devotions that he learned as a youngster laid the foundation for an adult faith that can withstand the setbacks and sorrows of life, but that also gives deeper meaning to life's greatest joys. In Kevin's story about learning to be a friend of Jesus, every reader, but men particularly, will find a compelling testimony to God's faithfulness and a source of encouragement as they seek to connect their daily lives to God and to trust in the power of prayer."

—Cardinal Donald Wuerl, Archbishop of Washington

"*Burst* is a profound meditation on reality. In his experience of unexpected and unwanted suffering, Kevin Wells encounters not only terrible pain but amazing grace. From the hands of a talented writer and the heart of a faithful believer comes this riveting tale of courage, resilience and faith. I cannot imagine anyone who will not be moved by this stunning story of surrender to God's grace. Highly recommended."

—Fr. James Martin, author of *My Life with the Saints*

"*Burst* offers a unique insight into human suffering, while leading the reader to theological reflection and the contemplation of grace. For Kevin Wells, this leads him to a deeper conversion of heart and mind—a natural following for anyone who reads his story."

—Fr. Leo E. Patalinghug, host and author of www.gracebeforemeals.com

"I knew Kevin when he was a sports writer, and even then I knew his words and his life would carry him far beyond playing fields and box scores. And anyone who reads this book is better for that. It's a story of near death and all that life can be, of tragedy and triumph, of God's love and the splendor of faith, of a shining light named Tommy, a savior named Krista and three gifts from heaven above named Gabrielle, Sean and Shannon. Someone once said, "Faith isn't faith until it's all you're holding onto." Kevin's words and story take you in like that, in a warm spiritual embrace that never lets go."

—Martin Fennelly, nationally-acclaimed
sports columnist for the *Tampa Tribune*

"Burst is a high-energy story demonstrating the goodness of God in all circumstances—tragic, joyful and miraculous—and even in the ordinary events of everyday life. As a former sports writer and avid sports fan, Mr. Wells understands that sports, like all of life, is most real when Jesus Christ is placed at its very core."

—Ray McKenna, founder and president of
Catholic Athletes for Christ

"As the story progresses, it becomes clear that what sets this family apart is the abundance of faithfulness, grace and obedience to the will of God. *Burst* is truly a beautiful witness to marriage and the domestic church. This should be required reading in every Pre-Cana curriculum as it is the story of what to do with the unexpected: Put it into the hands of God and pray."

—Michele Bowe

BURST

burst

A STORY OF GOD'S GRACE WHEN LIFE FALLS APART

Kevin Wells

SERVANT
BOOKS

PUBLISHED BY ST. ANTHONY MESSENGER PRESS
CINCINNATI, OHIO

Scripture texts in this work are taken from the *New American Bible with Revised New Testament and Revised Psalms* © 1991, 1986, 1970 Confraternity of Christian Doctrine, Washington, D.C. and are used by permission of the copyright owner. All Rights Reserved. No part of the *New American Bible* may be reproduced in any form without permission in writing from the copyright owner.

Cover and book design by Mark Sullivan
Cover photo © istockphoto.com | Alex Slobodkin

LIBRARY OF CONGRESS CATALOGING-IN-PUBLICATION DATA
Wells, Kevin B.
Burst : a story of God's grace when life falls apart / Kevin Wells.
p. cm.
Includes bibliographical references and index.
ISBN 978-0-86716-948-5 (pbk. : alk. paper) 1. Wells, Kevin B. 2. Brain--Surgery--Patients--Religious life. 3. Cerebral arteriovenous malformations--Surgery. I. Title. II. Title: Story of God's grace when life falls apart.
BV4910.W45 2011
248.8'619681--dc22
2010048502

ISBN 978-0-86716-948-5

Published by Servant Books, an imprint of St. Anthony Messenger Press.
28 W. Liberty St.
Cincinnati, OH 45202
www.AmericanCatholic.org
www.ServantBooks.org

Printed in the United States of America.

Printed on acid-free paper.

11 12 13 14 15 5 4 3 2 1

For Krista.
Thank you for sitting and waiting on God
to make it all go away.

contents

acknowledgments

This book took life due to mine almost ending. With that in mind, I want to heap bottomless gratitude on all those family-and-friend cheerleaders who stood vigil near my ICU room, praying for my brain to heal.

Thank you to acquisitions editor Cindy Cavnar at Servant Books, for gambling that an old sportswriter (of all things!) might have something to offer on God's grace in broken times. Not only did you guide *Burst* into being, Cindy; you've been my indispensable shepherd throughout this process. Also, editor Lucy Scholand—I doubt there are many better.

And this book could not have escaped its clumsiness without the vital, three-headed craft(wo)manship of Jennifer Brinker, Eileen Guerrin, and Susan Vogel. Your willingness to offer your considerable time, touch, and wisdom was instrumental in steering this book into port.

Mom and Dad, the warmest of thank-yous. All of your eight children are faithful Catholics today because of your selfless, unwavering model on how to live and love as Christ.

To each of my brothers and sisters: I've plucked unique bits of inspiration and example from each of you—even from you, Johnny. All of you are loved in a mighty way.

To my friend Fr. Jim Stack, what can I say? Thank you for anointing and saving me. A miracle happened that night— which is why I'm obliged to also thank my uncle, Msgr. Thomas "Tommy" Wells. When Stackman and I called, naturally, you lit up the room. I miss you, Tommy, but memories of your example have been a lantern as I walk this world.

To my children, Gabrielle, Sean, and Shannon. You are God's greatest indication that he loves me. Thank you for bringing such bright joy into my life.

This brings me to you, Krista. I've never doubted God gave us to each other. I marvel at your ability to continually shoulder the cross and navigate past the pain to find Christ's embrace. You pieced me back together. And until the cows come home, I am indebted.

F e r o c i o u s   L o v e

One plain evening a vine of vessels in my brain burst when I rested my head on my pillow for sleep. It was January 2, 2009, and that evening I had simply watched a movie with my children and read from a Michael O'Brien novel. Thereafter it seemed a tomahawk met my skull. Before I could reach for my wife, Krista, asleep beside me, blood was seeping into tight crevices within my cerebellum. My head was rapidly becoming a tankful of blood and other unwanted fluids.

Within moments of the pain's arrival, I realized it was accelerating. When I arose from bed to vomit, I couldn't walk a straight line to the bathroom. I managed to nudge Krista and whispered for her to call 911. The sirens awakened curious neighbors fifteen minutes later.

The emergency medical technician was holding up three fingers; I thought five. It was my brain, I knew. Man. My brain.

Upstairs Gabrielle, Sean, and Shannon were well into their kaleidoscopes of dreams. As I was tenderly carried by EMTs past small bowls of leftover popcorn, there came the thought that I might never reach for my children again.

Man.

I was hurried to a nearby hospital, where I was promptly given a CAT scan. I was lying on a gurney in a fit of severe head pain, throwing up into a small pan while awaiting the results, when a friendly, youngish-looking male nurse approached.

"Hey there, man," he greeted me with kind eyes. "I don't know everything there is to know about reading CATs, but I think you're gonna be OK. I didn't see anything out of the ordinary."

In what seemed a second later, a doctor approached with my scan to inform me otherwise. Pointing to the malformation of veins and arteries in the rear of my skull that had started the release of blood into my brain, he named it an arteriovenous malformation. He said I was in the midst of an intracranial brain hemorrhage and that I needed to be taken immediately to a different hospital. I looked to the nurse in the corner of the room and saw the twin expression of shame and sorrow.

I was rushed to the University of Maryland Medical Center, an enormous building wedged into a cozy shot-and-beer section of downtown Baltimore and an easy stroll from a ballpark where I once covered major league baseball games as a sportswriter. Two solemn EMTs opened the back doors of the ambulance, and the bracingly cold winds, walled in by the surrounding buildings, momentarily allowed me to ignore the tomahawk.

Shortly after my admission into the intensive care unit, I began having hallucinations—images that seemed to have been created, signed off, and delivered by a raging chorus of demons. I repeatedly saw my seven-year-old daughter, Gabby, drowning in a shallow, flowing stream of water in the ceiling tiles above. When I attempted to save her and found myself unable to move due to my restrained arms, I was mocked by the revolting forms that had taken up hallucinogenic real estate within the undulating tiles.

One gyrating, multi-headed monster shrugged its shoulders and swept its translucent hands toward my daughter, seemingly saying, "What of it, Kevin? Gonna save her or what, man?"

The image seemed as real as the oversized clock that ticked in the right corner of the room. I repeatedly asked Krista to stand on my bed to get to our drowning daughter trapped beyond the tiles. But she just kept sweeping my forehead, like a mother soothing her sick child to sleep.

Once lucid, I realized that little was working in my favor. The shunts launched into my skull to remove the excess fluids kept clotting. Once Krista was told by a neurosurgeon who stopped by at the right time, "Kevin might die if we don't insert another shunt right now."

"OK, insert one," said Krista.

Over the next few weeks, Krista would stand sentinel by my side unless she was asked to leave. When not at my bedside, she would sleep on a small wooden chair in the lobby. She often awoke in the lonely hours of the morning, and she would look through the lobby door's glass panel to make sure my room was still dark. She learned that a well-lit room during the night shift meant that surgeons were likely in there working wildly.

Within a few days I couldn't form a sentence. Two angiograms to survey my brain's condition didn't spring cheery news. It would be unwieldy getting to the puddled blood, which by hell or high water needed to be absorbed as soon as possible. It was decided by the chief neurosurgeon to open the back of my head and operate. His goal: to untangle and obliterate the wild nest of veins and arteries and relieve the mounting pressure within my head.

After hours of penetration, though, the procedure turned awkward. The surgeon laid his instruments down and left the operating table. Minutes later a gathering of my brothers, cousins, and friends were summoned from a subdued Pickles Pub down the street, where they had assembled to keep vigil. They quietly set down their pints of good-luck Guinness, stepped into the frigid January night, and zombied north toward the hospital.

Meanwhile, Krista and Mom and Dad and a separate gathering of friends and relatives were pulled from the hospital's "Healing Garden" to meet with my surgeon. On the walk down the long, polished corridor, prayers for recovery intensified.

In short order the considerable group of my muted cheerleaders stood in stern solidarity in a narrow room, where many anticipated the gravest of news. But my surgeon, a serious-minded man from South Africa, assured them I was alive. He carefully explained that fully penetrating the cerebellum or navigating around it to get to the disordered archipelago of bleeding veins and arteries and recalcitrant blood could cause serious residual damage or instant death. He had to stop.

Options were thinning.

Shortly after awakening from surgery, my friend Fr. Rob Walsh was called in to administer the sacrament of the anointing of the sick, and I started thinking about judgment. Two other priests who are friends offered to hear my whispered confessions. "Bless me, Father; it's been three hours since my last confession...." The clock in the corner ticked as family and old high school friends kept tiptoeing into my dark, shoe-box–sized room, smiling at me like a kindergartner at his first picture-taking.

"Hey, Kevin," some whispered into my right ear. "So whaddaya think? Are the Ravens gonna beat the Titans this weekend?"

"Somebody get to Gabby," I whispered, words that confused them.

It was then, when circumstances were grim as Gethsemane, that Christ zigzagged in.

The Last Supper

During my college years I was invited into a three-generation family tradition of spending a winter weekend at an old Jesuit retreat house buried in the thick of the forest, bordering gentle southern Maryland farmland. The sprawling maroon-brick estate rests footsteps from a steep cliff that overlooks a strikingly broad expanse of the Potomac River. I'd be hard-pressed to find a more peaceful spot on the eastern seaboard of America. Sunsets there have made tough men cry.

I was taught there by learned, kind Jesuits the uncommon power and intensity of contemplative prayer. For five hundred years Jesuits have made prayerful contemplation the sustaining centerpiece of their spiritual lives. They will tell you that Christ can be revealed to you in a host of profound ways by practicing the Spiritual Exercises introduced by the Society of Jesus' daring founder, St. Ignatius of Loyola. Within the exercises (which, if you're game, can be practiced for thirty successive days of silence), men and women are led by a spiritual director into an intense period of prayer and meditation that centers on sin and the life, passion, death, and resurrection of Jesus. The aim of the exercises is to have retreatants reflect on the encounters they've had with Christ in their meditations and to discern how those meetings might deepen their relationship with Christ.

In truncated form, here's what the Jesuits have suggested to me over the years: Find a quiet spot (it's easy, because the retreat house and grounds are as noiseless as Pluto), close my eyes, and spend some time slowly breathing. Gradually, when I consider it appropriate, imagine Christ present beside me, breathing life into me and all that surrounds me. Take a few minutes, the Jesuits direct in a voice softer than wood smoke, and become truly aware of Christ's presence. After a few minutes of assessing my state of mind, they ask that I slowly read one Gospel passage and gradually, as unobtrusively as possible, introduce myself into the scene.

I had been on retreat at the blessed Jesuit retreat house exactly one month prior to my brain hemorrhage. There I closed my eyes, engaged in the deep-breathing preliminaries, and tread softly into the scene of my Scripture passage. On this occasion I was alone in an unlit corner of the Upper Room. I looked around and saw a plain table with a few dimly lit candles under a low ceiling. A small wafer of moonlight fell upon the dusty floor. A chill hung in the air.

Eventually I watched the thick wooden door swing open and an assortment of rough-edged, hungry men enter. Jesus was among them, fitting in but not really fitting in. After some time the men settled in for a Passover feast. Small talk began to blanket the unfamiliar room. Some questioned the purpose behind gathering at a strange place on such a significant night. A few men prepared the meal, while others sneaked glances at Jesus, who returned their looks with an unnatural smile.

After some time I watched Jesus step away from the table. He tied a clean rag around his waist and reached for a large basin. He filled it with the water the men were supposed to be drinking. Then he knelt before the man closest to the door.

Talk between the men softened, and eventually the room fell wordless. I watched Jesus remove the filth from the feet of his friends. Only one man, Peter, cracked the silence with his bluster over Christ's startling act of humility—telling Jesus he would never wash his feet—but Christ deflected his noisy plea and then moved on down the long line of awestruck men.

From my dark corner I saw Jesus silently teaching his friends yet another facet of love. The aorta of the group— their remarkable leader—was on his knees tending to their filth with palms that would soon be shredded. His hands were steady as he tenderly washed away the dirt. Hours from his agony, he was calm.

This is the soft genius of Ignatian contemplation. I was there to see everything unfold and then depart from the encounter with enlightenment into how Christ was working within my own life.

Perhaps some see this brand of harnessed imagination as blasphemous or scandalous, but for centuries wise men have allowed the practice to imbue their spiritual lives, and they have seemed holier and happier for it. The method has helped me forge a closer intimacy with Christ.

So from my hospital bed, I closed my eyes and returned to it. Christ came differently this time though.

First he maneuvered past the wild beehive of demons above. And like the quarterback who heads for the locker room touching fans' arms, hands, and shoulders on the way, Christ touched my smoldering head, full-body pain, and swollen joints and kept moving. He touched the terror, the wounded psyche, the loneliness, and the Job-like vulnerability.

After a while he rested. At perhaps the solitary place in my mind that still operated with orderly function, he began making things well.

He sat down against a perfectly rounded, stout boulder in a field of poppies and long swaying grass greener than sun-splashed Killarney hillsides. Seven or so children, aged five to eight, encircled him as softly as incense hovers in cathedral light. Some knelt before him, praying. One smiling girl hugged his neck from behind. Some sat cross-legged, heads cocked, looking adoringly into his sunlit, lightly bearded face.

And there I was, sprawled pathetically at his feet, peculiar and unfit for the scene. I had multiple IVs crisscrossing my arms and tubes shooting out of my partially shaved, scarred, bloody head. Wearing my flimsy, smelly hospital garb and too weak to kneel, I lay my broken head in his lap and watched my tears spill onto his cloak. He took one hand and lightly, so lightly, placed it on my seven-inch scar.

Christ didn't say a word to me. And the joyful cast of children didn't seem to notice the afflicted outsider butting in on their time with the Lord in the dazzling countryside. He entertained them in a language I wasn't permitted to know or perhaps couldn't due to my condition. Jesus' face brightened as he smiled, and he often laughed as the children adored and comforted him.

An artist would have blocked me out were he to paint the portrait. But Jesus' hand remained fixed to my broken head. And soon I thought, I could be well.

For a long time my mind held on to the scene. I stared into the pastureland from my 90-degree head angle, and strong-stemmed red poppies lurched upward through the luminous lake of green, saying, "You must rise too."

So I did.

The bleeding was absorbed, the fluids drained freely, and the shadows behind my eyes dispersed. At least one nurse called the overnight absorption of blood a miracle. Then others agreed.

I would learn later of something else that occurred in my ICU room that night.

Home Again

Three weeks later I made it home. I have a vivid if unspectacular memory of that time.

Unable to get around, I lay in bed and stared into an industrial-white bedroom ceiling. I caught the whiff of the meal Krista was preparing for dinner downstairs, where six-year-old Sean was screaming something from the family room that I couldn't or didn't want to understand. Tiny Shannon was napping, and Gabby was reading from another of her Geronimo Stilton books alongside me. Family life, I thought. Jackpot.

I was alive.

Because my cerebellum had been cut, my equilibrium, coordination, and sight were as steady as Belushi's at 3 AM. For the first time in my life I wore glasses when I tried to read. My handwriting bore a resemblance to that of my Uncle Al when he wrote to me from a poorly lit parlor in Perry, Georgia. But he was 103, and I was 41 in good lighting. If I reached for the *R* on the keyboard of my laptop, I had a 50-50 shot at it; often it was the *E* I got.

My head felt waterlogged all the time. Headaches came like mini guillotines, and I often felt as if there was an elf carving away at something in the center of my head.

I would be bedridden for some time. I was told the issues were routine stuff and would improve. My neurosurgeon told me I would be back to my old self in a year or so. Yet that wasn't really the point. It would have been a shame if it was.

I'm hardly a masochist, but I really believe my close call with death and the residual array of significant inconveniences should prove helpful, perhaps soul-saving even. Think of it as purgatory time already served. I believe much of the acute, lasting pain I've accumulated throughout my life has arrived as a sort of message from God, kind of like a postcard dropped from heaven that's as heavy as an anvil.

I am just fragile and thoughtless enough to frequently get lost in the tangle of life and plow forward, doing what I suppose many others do: wake up, make coffee, work with the discipline my Dad instilled, drive home, throw a laughing child in the air, talk to my wife about the day, read, pray, go to bed. Not good enough. Anvil time.

The audacious, brilliant detail that I used to overlook with the anvil was that it landed with love. A ferocious love.

I'm finding out that God's love really doesn't seek consolation; it seeks total intimacy. And because his desire for loving union with me is unrelenting, his tender reach may occasionally come across as rather fierce. He can love with boxing gloves. And perhaps it's his very best brand of love—because his punches are loaded with hard shots of salvific grace that rouse me from my slumber and help escort me back to proper and absolute unity with him. If I oblige with a whispered yes on these occasions, my cooperation with his grace invitations inches my soul closer to precious exclusivity with him.

Some graces land soft as autumn shadows; others break in like bulldozers unearthing tough ground, to shake loose the multilayered sufferings of our souls. Grace can arrive like a trombone blast or glide in unannounced, unnoticed, and unprayed for. It is God's greatest indication that he loves us and wants us to be united with him in every facet of our lives. Remarkably grace is God—his charity, his love, his very presence—cracked open and alive within us.

Even when that grace seems to grind us into submission.

GRACED SUFFERERS

The line of saints who've suffered is, paradoxically, a long and cheerful one. St. Paul became Christianity's greatest missionary and evangelist, with a harassing "thorn" as his unremitting travel companion (see 2 Corinthians 10:7). And perhaps the most lasting souvenir from St. Peter's time with Christ was the revolting knowledge that he had denied him. But he bore that hounding psychological cross and became the rock on which Christ built his church.

Much later St. Rose of Lima, the first saint of the Americas, said that if we understood how suffering leads us to Christ, we would beg him for more. Sweet St. Thérèse of Lisieux, racked with emotional trials, tuberculosis, and spiritual dryness for extended periods of her short life, said, "The cross has accompanied me from the cradle, but then, Jesus has made me love it passionately."[1] As I type these words, there are perhaps hundreds of worn-out souls pleading for her intercession—or for a rose or two to spring up in the backyard.

St. Faustina Kowalska, who watched many days unfold from inside a sanatorium, said, "Sufferings, adversities, failures and suspicions that have come my way are splinters that keep alive the fire of my love for You, O Jesus."[2]

Heaven knows I am no saint (ask every single person who has ever known me), but it's my goal to become one—as it should be for each of us. My heartache and discomfort—and there had been a fair amount even prior to my brain troubles—have been the perfect beacon, I think, from an Abba-Father who wants unreserved unity with me. I don't think this paternal God has chosen to inject suffering into my life for pure sport or to harass me. I do believe, though, that along with desiring greater intimacy, he's allowed pain in my life in hopes that I'll gain a greater understanding of the cross. It's when I avoid the cross that I become more worldly and distant, like a Prodigal Son who decides to continue hiding away.

But fortunately, like the Prodigal Son, who managed to hold on to his precious pinhole of awareness, I have found that my suffering has often reconstructed and humbled me and caused my thoughts to rocket back to my Father. It's then—through that union of prayer and intimacy—that my cross meets his. And then my pain begins to serve a purpose.

To attain that true intimacy, he asks that I both consecrate the pain to him and die to the stubborn parts of me that resist. The intimacy is the pearl of great price, and surrender and change often seem beyond my reach—like riding a bicycle to the moon. But if I oblige, my suffering becomes purposeful, and his glory is magnified. In a tiny part of the universe, Christ's grand message of love grows a bit—which is wonderful for me and those around me. It means that grace is slowly taking root—perfecting nature, in fact—and that his kingdom is growing a bit.

In his apostolic letter *Salvifici Doloris,* Pope John Paul II wrote that "suffering must serve for conversion, that is for the rebuilding of goodness in the subject."[3] Every bit of my pain—at least what I would consider to be profound, life-altering pain—had better trigger change and spiritual maturity within me. Everything in life happens for a reason, including our anvils.

Perhaps that's why when the anvil's landed, it hasn't buried me. In fact, it's often sprung renewal.

chapter two

Quiet Hero , Quiet Town

The wire story came across one winter night, which didn't seem like winter because temperatures were in the low eighties, and Santa Claus was wearing silk shorts in the Winter Haven Mall: "The Cleveland Indians announced the free-agent signing of veteran first baseman Eddie Murray today."

Man. The luck. My childhood hero, the only one, was coming to the very town I was about to flee.

The Indians' spring training home was in Winter Haven, Florida, which was also my home this winter of 1994. If I stayed in town, my job would be to cover Murray and his teammates, which included all-stars Albert Belle, Kenny Lofton, and cocksure rookie Manny Ramirez.

The winds of change were about to descend.

THE MOVE SOUTH

After college I had moved into a downtown Baltimore row house with four good friends. The place was a half block from Babe Ruth's birthplace and across the street from the

Orioles' spectacular new ballpark. We used to sit on our stoop and eavesdrop on the crowd noise while exchanging hellos with some of the all-black patrons strolling into Strike Three, the aged corner bar that was attached to one end of our row house. I befriended some bar regulars and one of its owners, a huge man named Bill, who used to serve me fried macaroni with a large bottle of Schlitz malt liquor.

I had a decent reporter's job at a respectable weekly newspaper and moonlighted at Orioles games as a lemonade man. Other than the dozen or so cartoon-sized city rats that lived with us, a meager-paying full-time job, and an indulgence in a mediocre Orioles team, life rolled by at a leisurely, pleasant pace. It wasn't hard to see even then that I was postponing adulthood. I knew I needed to uproot to further my goal of becoming a beat writer at a major daily newspaper.

I arranged interviews with seven newspapers on a two-week job-search journey to the Deep South. The job I least wanted was with *ehT sweN feihC* (I've scrambled the letters of the newspaper to keep its identity underground), partly because of the unsettling night I spent in the country town where the daily was published.

I had pulled into the 1,000 Lakes Motel, which looked like the 10 Lakes Motel at night because two large bulbs had blown out. I shared my room with two lizards until I mentioned it to the manager, who came to my room in a huff to end their lives with the bottom of his sandal. This slaughter happened just a few hours after my interview with my future sports editor.

I had asked where I could find a place for dinner, and

someone had mentioned a restaurant downtown. Only I never found what I would consider a downtown (I later learned I had driven through the heart of it), so I ended up getting a sandwich at a Publix and taking it back to the 1,000 Lakes Motel, which had dropped 990 of its lakes due to nightfall. From my room I read that day's edition of the paper and swallowed a lot.

Three weeks later I pulled into the newspaper parking lot as an employee—my car still piping hot and crammed with all my belongings after a sixteen-hour trip. I was greeted by my new editor with "I thought you were gonna be here yesterday.... Don't spend any time with the girls in Classifieds. The last guy was let go because of that."

Then he asked me to cover a volleyball match in Frostproof, a godforsaken town in the middle of nowhere and an hour south of Winter Haven—also a town I considered in the middle of nowhere, just a little less so. He handed me a reporter's notepad and some handwritten directions. I got back into my poor little teal Toyota to extend my trip to Frostproof, which had a population of a single person to every one million oranges.

After turning in my volleyball story later that evening, I hurried to find a new home. I found one at the Brandywine Apartments, a set of fifteen or so spruced-up brown trailers that had been unloaded onto a barren, open field on a poor end of town. My rectangular, one-bedroom unit was surrounded by one of those one thousand lakes, an orange grove, and a convalescent center. The median age of my neighbors was that of Moses.

My Baltimore stoop was nine hundred miles north.

Because of my moonlight working hours, I wasn't able to establish any friendships. I missed Thanksgiving at home for the first time, spending it instead in the country home of a newspaper clerk. A fistfight between quarrelsome men in Wranglers and creased Nascar caps broke out in her small front yard. The brawl put a dent in the holiday merrymaking, so the paper plates and half-eaten hot dogs and cranberry sauce were thrown out. But the memorable evening did give me something to write about for the paper.

After a few months with *ehT sweN feihC,* I was looking for a way out. A large color illustration of an Indian warrior festooned the paper's masthead, and a warpath of typos and other errors bled into the pages that followed. It was tagged by locals as "the fish wrap," and it was a difficult task to ever catch townsfolk reading it.

I worked the night shift with a few other writers, and I was repeatedly instructed to help fill the entire front page of the sports section with local news—and local news only! If Wayne Gretzky had hijacked a rocket ship and steered it toward Neptune alongside copilot Mike Tyson, it would have been buried on the inside pages.

Because local sports news often was in short supply, I used to walk a Little League baseball complex—Sertoma Park, I'll never forget—and strike up conversations with field maintenance workers, hot dog vendors, T-ball players, proud grandpops, whoever had a working voice box. The following day the unsuspecting "local personality" would have metamorphosed into a screaming, front-page, top-of-the-fold news story. Newsworthiness be damned, I had column space to fill.

So I filled it, writing like Bigfoot. And as my writing and reporting degenerated, I saw my major-daily dreams begin to fragment and then plunge into a full-scale dilapidation of spirit and ambition. It was time to leave and perhaps find a new way of earning a living.

Then Eddie came.

THE BREAK

On summer vacations in the New Hampshire mountains, my older brother Danny and I would make nightly appointments to listen to Orioles games from the front seat of our wood-paneled station wagon. As moonlit Lake Winnipesaukee's crickets and bullfrogs harmonized, we fiddled with the radio dial with a watchmaker's touch until we managed to pull the crackle of WBAL flagship announcers Bill O'Donnell and Chuck Thompson, who would bring to life the latest glories of Eddie Murray. We often lost contact as their voices detoured into the traffic of other nighttime radio men, but we would sit like eager purgatory souls—fiddling, fiddling, fiddling——until their cadenced whispers came back like a three-days-dead Lazarus.

We heard Memorial Stadium's blue-collar symphony serenade Murray with its riotous, singsong hymn of adoration—"Ed-die! Ed-die! Ed-die!"—which ricocheted off the narrow Waverly row houses that wrapped around the old neighborhood ballpark like a protective mother bear. And Murray, the greatest clutch hitter in the game, seemed to always oblige by waving a bat and sending a baseball to a part of the field no one had thought to cover. I used to imagine sleepers all over the quiet city enclave being awakened when Murray found a way yet again to deliver during a late-inning crisis.

Baltimore loved its quiet hero. And Eddie loved the town back. I would have grown his Afro if able.

But the pendulum had swung since the days when I would summon "Murray courage" to wrap my arm around a girl's shoulder in a movie theatre. Once a beguiling, charming prankster, Murray had developed into a veteran skeptical of all reporters. He had been criticized by an Orioles owner in an article in the mid-eighties, which had opened the door for media members to nitpick. Thereafter he initiated an unbending stonewalling of the press. Catchwords—"lazy," "clubhouse cancer," "The Frown Prince"—began to append themselves to him, all the while he was evolving into one of baseball's most feared hitters.

His best friends said Murray's derogatory tags were entirely unjustified. One whom I knew said Murray was a kind, thoughtful individual who loved the game of baseball but had been mischaracterized simply because of his firm decision to wall himself off from the media. This friend also told me that Murray wouldn't speak with me.

So on the opening day of spring training, I walked up to him.

It was mid-February, and gusty winds were whipping off another one of those one thousand lakes beside the Kelly-green, cloverleafed baseball fields. Eddie seemed to be in good spirits. He had just finished a light morning workout, his first as a member of the Indians. He was walking back to the clubhouse when I greeted the man I used to sketch in my grade-school notebooks.

"Eddie, if you wouldn't mind, do you have a few minutes?" I asked. "I'm Kevin Wells with the local paper."

"Nah. I'm sorry," he said politely as he continued toward the clubhouse.

"I promise, if you give me a minute or two, you'll see that I'm not here to knock you," I said.

"I'm sorry," he said with a smile. "I'm just not talking."

And he walked on.

DAY TWO

"Hey, 33," I said in the same location a day later.

"Man, what's up with you?" he asked with a bemused look.

Murray stopped this time though. Progress.

"Eddie, I know more about your career than any baseball writer in America. I, uh, can say that with confidence. All I want to do is profile you for our spring training magazine that comes out next week. It won't be a hammer job.... I mean, c'mon, I'm with the local paper."

He smiled. "How do you think you know me so well?"

I could have told him that he awed me as a child. I could have told him how I used to hop atop my bed and pantomime his crouched, cobra-like batting stance in my pajamas while listening to WBAL in the dark. I could have explained that I chose to attend Loyola College near Memorial Stadium just to see him play. I could have mentioned that I would have grown his Afro if able.

"I grew up in Maryland as an Orioles fan," I offered. "I know how you play the game. I've followed your career."

"I'm sorry. I just don't speak with you guys," he said.

"Eddie," I said. "As a kid, believe it or not, you were my favorite player."

"Oh, man," he said, laughing. "What have I got myself into here?... Your parents should have told you to like somebody else—like Cal or somebody."

"Yeah, you're probably right," I said with a smile.

"Sorry, Kevin," he said.

"Eddie, look. I'm with the local paper. Even if I write something awful about you, maybe a dozen or so people will even see it," I bargained.

"You're not gonna give up, are you?" he asked.

"Eddie, I live in Winter Haven," I said. "What else have I got to do?"

"All right," he said with his famous high-pitched laugh. "Meet me in the clubhouse in ten minutes."

We spoke for a memorable hour at his locker. He discussed his poor Los Angeles childhood, his enormous love for his large family, and learning how to hit curveballs by swinging at Crisco lids as a kid. He talked of "the Orioles Way," the damning quotes, his hurts, his friendships with Lee May, Elrod Hendricks, Al Bumbry, and Cal Ripken, and his regret that he was no longer in Baltimore, a city he had come to love. "The thing that killed me was the 'sources say,'" he said with a touch of sadness in his dark eyes. "There's no doubt in my mind that none of my teammates said anything bad about me."

After the interview I walked into the media room, and

Paul Hoynes, the Indians beat writer for the *Cleveland Plain Dealer,* pivoted from his laptop and asked, "How in the &%$#* did you get Murray to talk?"

As the spring moved forward, Eddie and I established a short-lived friendship—discussing the NCAA basketball tournament, Baltimore restaurants, old Orioles stories, and the baseball minutiae of the day. Then Eddie left town to start the baseball season. And I went back to Sertoma Park and my hot dog vendors.

Laundry-room IBM

The luxurious thing about despairing situations, I've found, is the suddenly more pronounced stance Christ takes. And in the spring of '94, I had a growing hunger to be lost completely in him. My dependence, coffin career, and thinning rays of hope I lay tenderly in his lap in prayer. Of course, that was easy to do. What made that time in my life so meaningful was what accompanied my prayer life— the Great Silence.

Because I was poor, I had no television set or music player—other than my old clock radio, which picked up a few of the country and bluegrass stations I neglected. I'd wake to silence, eat in silence, go to bed in silence. For the first time I tasted the otherworldly embrace of solitude and stillness.

Initially the Cistercian quietude was unsettling, but gradually I grew accustomed to it, and eventually the peace became a resplendent tool. It was within that unwavering embrace of stillness—and honestly, loneliness, discouragement, and isolation were in that brown trailer with me too—that I found the mysterious presence of God through ever-silent prayer, always accompanied by an old-fashioned monstrosity of a personal computer.

Here's how my prayer time unfolded: Before work each day I sat down in front of the mammoth IBM, which hummed continuously in my home office (located in my narrow washer- and dryer-less laundry room) and unloaded letters to God in a self-righteous mope, as if I had a justifiable claim to a Christ-created escape hatch. God, how in the world did I end up here? What am I gonna do about this? Oh, boy, God, I just wrote a twenty-inch article on a junior varsity volleyball game! God, I'm writing to you in a laundry room!

I wrote in a manner that was somehow despairing and prideful in equal proportions. But worse, my letters to God were little more than a disillusioned pile of wasted prayers.

Funny thing though about silence. In time it extracts pathetic musings to clear out space for a better annunciation of the Holy Spirit's voice. It's hard to be a self-pitying boor in a world where only silence speaks. The echoes of the noiselessness, which were louder than rifle shots, eventually drew open the curtains to a more precise awareness of the circumstances I had forged for myself.

I began to see that the small daily paper was probably the right spot for me. My writing, interviewing, and reporting skills were unspectacular, major dailies weren't hiring because of a lingering recession, and I was still rather young, at twenty-five years of age. I had a long way to go, and I knew God had a history of moving things along slowly.

A truer picture of my day-to-day experience began to emerge on my computer screen, which had become like an empty stretch of more contemplative highway prayers:

> Lord I'm alone in this country town. Write your story into my story, so at least then I'll be an instrument living out your will.
>
> You're not my personal genie in a bottle. You're my Good Shepherd. I know it will take time, and in your time you'll work it out.
>
> You know I'm in trouble here. Speak to my soul. I surrender my loneliness to you now, as the lepers did, while I try to persevere in this dry time. I'm a clumsy, anxious follower who awaits.
>
> Be the breath of my prayer. Amen.

I began to pray-write like a happy trailer-park hermit, realizing the "not yet" of my career might never be. Hope was the constant theme. And I began to hear him more clearly, because after all, it wasn't really me orchestrating all the jazzed-up fecundity in my prayer life; it was the Holy Spirit. "The Spirit too comes to the aid of our weakness; for we do not know how to pray as we ought, but the Spirit itself intercedes with inexpressible groanings" (Romans 8:26).

The time bomb of my writing career didn't tick, tick, tick as noisily when I placed my dilemma in his hands. Sure, I was in the heart of the proverbial desert (and one could argue the same in a literal sense), but it was within that hermetically sealed Polk County desert that I found prayer to be a mini paradise of self-awareness. Within the stillness I started to grasp that only patient acceptance and trust in his providence were adequate. And in my loneliness— by far my toughest challenge—I found his embrace by placing my temptations toward frustration, hopelessness, impatience, and the rest within his inexhaustible love. All I had was faith, and that seemed like an awful lot at the time.

WALKIN' AFTER MIDNIGHT, SEARCHIN' FOR YOU

I usually didn't get out of work until around eleven o'clock, which hampered meeting my neighbors. By the time I pulled up to my Tootsie-Roll–colored trailer, they were wallowing in ocean-deep REM sleep. After reading for a while, I'd walk into the warm night air for what became a fine ritual. There was a gravel road that ran near the bank of the lake behind my trailer. I'd pray the rosary or simply whisper the story of my day to God, as the splashes of mullets, frogs, tree storks, alligators, and egrets in Lake No-Name echoed all around.

I knew I was reaching out to God in prayer only because of God's gentle draw. Nothing I prayed was pious or lofty. He knew my story well; I told him anyway. The midnight examination-of-conscience walk uncluttered my mind and enabled a deeper introspection. In silence it was easy to access my failures, target my recurring shortcomings, chart my course for the following day, and finally welcome minute measures of hope.

Although all doors to a bright future seemed closed, I knew in my depths that they were wide open—no matter what spun out of my circumstances. Although I was living in a friendless wilderness, his paradise was all around me—sacramentalized in the highly visible constellations, the hoot of owls, the lapping of small lake waves. And although I worked at a thin newspaper that averaged six typos a page, well, there was only so much I could polish on those walks. Of course my heart remained restless, but it was repeatedly soothed through prayer.

The stubborn, God-given, theological virtue of hope—marvelous, faint, and oft-forgotten hope—accompanied me like an egging-on angel on those walks. I'll never forget how even a thimbleful of it managed to warm my soul with flash bonfires of peace. "[Hope] we have as an anchor of the soul, sure and firm, which reaches into the interior behind the veil" (Hebrews 6:19).

There was no manipulating God in prayer, I knew, but I could pour out to him the Spirit-inspired voice of my soul. I knew the lonesomeness of honey-voiced Patsy Cline's midnight walk too well, and I whispered my own lyrics aloud to the night sky.

> Lord, I am yours in this midnight moonlight. I have all the time in the world for you, all the space, all the desire for your unvoiced voice to speak to me on this road.
>
> I open my heart and mind to you. Speak, just as you spoke to your adrift apostles during their slow-motion awakening to your booming reality.
>
> With your voice directing my path, I have a way—your way.
>
> If I listen.

My ears are willing. If only I could hear your voice.

In the meantime may your name be glorified throughout this seeming mess.

Amen.

The executive sports editor from the *Tampa Tribune*, the late Paul C. Smith, called one evening to offer me a correspondent's position at one of the Tribune's bureaus in Lakeland. He said that if I worked hard and showed some talent and initiative, he would hire me full-time.

He had read the long article on Murray that was published in our paper. "You seem to really love baseball. Murray too. Well done," he said.

I was at a major daily.

Man.

chapter three

P o o f

During my year in Winter Haven, the thing that hounded me most was the unremitting loneliness. I didn't care about dating; I just wanted to spend time with a friend. So although I was thrilled to start my new job with the *Tampa Tribune*, I was also looking to resuscitate my flat-lined social life.

I moved into the bottom floor of a charming, two-story bungalow rented from an elderly Southern-fried lady named Ms. Montgomery. Located in Lakeland's pleasant historic district, my new home was a short walk from Florida Southern College, swan-graced Lake Morton, and Vito's, a delicious Italian restaurant built in the 1950s.

On the first day after moving in, I met Rich Lopez, who lived in the bungalow above. And life took off.

Rich, a Lakeland native, was a high school biology teacher, the son of Cuban immigrants, and the funniest person I had ever met. He was also kind and generous and perhaps the finest Christian I had come across. Everything he did seemed to be rooted in love with the intention to promote joy in others. It was his humor, though, that I appreciated most.

I made a fatal error in confiding to Rich that a girl named Elise had broken my heart prior to my move to Florida. So at various times throughout the ensuing months, he tilted his enormous speaker toward his bungalow floorboards and played the Cure's "Letter to Elise" at a decibel that may have awakened my old trailer neighbors twenty-five miles east of us.

Our seventy-some-year-old next-door neighbor, Ms. Ruth, ran a tiny business out of her house that she called "Ruth's ThreadBears." She would take the old clothing of a customer and knit it into a teddy bear. Rich let Ms. Ruth know that I, too, had been a knitter but had stopped altogether because I was mourning the loss of an old girlfriend named Elise. It took some time for me to figure out why Ms. Ruth kept tapping on my screen door to share tales of ThreadBear knitting with me. And she would look me in the eye with the tenderness of the Blessed Mother as she placed her hand on my forearm with empathy and compassion.

Rich invited me on alligator hunts, to his parents' home for Cuban feasts, and to the best spots in Ybor City and Orlando. I was welcomed full-bore into the abundant life he had forged; all his old friends became my new ones. Some nights we sipped beers on his small porch above my bungalow—leisurely reclined on the sturdy cedar Adirondack chairs he'd built—and swap stories about our relationships with God, our intended futures, the troubling souvenirs of our past, our dream brides, all of it. Those nights formed cherished memories. It was as if they were an answered prayer.

My Dream Bride Comes Riding

It was around this time that I began to visit a wide-open land lonelier than the moon. I would settle in behind scrub and heavy weeds along a winding, two-lane country road. There I would watch a charming collision of wills unfold, as my future wife and a puzzled horse aired their hostilities on a sun-scorched pasture under an enormous blue sky.

Spread around me were acres of farmland, where cattle chewed their cud and dined on the occasional patch of surviving grass. Large birds flew low, flies buzzed, and half a dozen kittens spread out seeking cool shadows beneath enormous, crooked live oak trees. The breeze that occasionally passed through drew brief, two-note dings from the wind chime hooked to a rafter inside Krista's small wooden barn.

The only dominant noise—the one that cracked the silence and kept me hiding like a creep in the weeds—was the cadenced clomp of an enraged thoroughbred at half-gallop. Quiet Krista would hold the reigns, and as she embarked on her campaign of reform against a sweat-slickened horse named Bowie, I was falling in love.

I marveled at her work. She could take a broken-down horse that couldn't win, place, or show at downtrodden Tampa Bay Downs—the doormat of America's thoroughbred racetracks—and resurrect his sleeping spirit with the nonchalance of a girl smoothing the hem of her skirt. In short order the broken horse would become a young child's future champion hunter-jumper.

But before hints of promise began to take root in Bowie, there was confusion in that meadow. I'd roll in the weeds in laughter as Krista repeatedly approached a meager jump at full trot, only to have the horse slow to a stop, twist his head aggressively, and snort and whinny like Veruca Salt on an especially bad day. The lumbering ritual unfolded in monotonous, torturous fashion: Krista would unleash hard kicks to hind legs and reverse course; the horse would buck as if he'd been shot and dart angrily back to his starting point by the entrance to the barn.

Finally I watched the poor animal step gingerly over the piece of plastic PVC pipe that passed for a jump. And as the day plodded along under the high sun, he began to leap awkwardly over more challenging jumps.

A week or so later (I was out of the scrub now), that seemingly feeble-minded horse was a hulking, disciplined, half-ton beast. He seemed to have grown a switchblade for a heart, obliging each of Krista's whispered commands. In harmony and sync the pair soared over more elegant arrangements of jumps, like an eagle in flight over towering treetops.

The humiliating losses and ill treatment at Tampa Bay Downs were forgotten, and that thoroughbred ran as if his life depended on it. He now believed, I suppose, with all the horse sense he could summon, that he was born and bred to be a champion hunter-jumper.

I had competed in various team sports since I was a small child, but Krista possessed the vital athletic traits I lacked: patience and grace. She would be tested.

The Beginning

I met Krista one night at a Bennigan's in the heart of the Florida Bible Belt. It was a warm autumn night in 1996, and I had just beat deadline for a Lake Wales–Haines City high school football game when I went in for a beer. She was standing by the horseshoe of the bar with some friends. Immediately I noticed she was shy—unlike a girl named "Bunny" whom I had recently dated but decided to hop, hop, hop away from.

Bennigan's lighting isn't great, yet I noticed the shine in Krista's long brown hair and her hazel eyes. She covered her full lips with dark lipstick; she had the Italian glow and an impenetrable beauty. But it was her nature that drew me.

I hadn't said a word to her, but I was taken by her apparent gentleness. She allowed her two friends, Erin and Cori, to direct the conversation I couldn't hear from my spot ten or so feet away. Krista smiled, laughed, and spoke every so often as she touched Cori's shoulder with noticeable warmth and consideration.

After a while I mustered the courage to say something breathtakingly stupid about her eyes to get her to talk. She bit but told me my line was awful. Then, in a clumsy parking-lot conversation beneath a blanket of stars, she told me that her life was horses, that she was Catholic, and that her family owned the two Italian restaurants in town.

Our first date was Sunday Mass two days later. Nervousness prevented us from making eye contact until the kiss of peace. After Mass we dined at Fat Jack's, an old Lakeland restaurant that still serves a decent fried-everything breakfast. Over a cup of strong coffee and buttered grits, she mentioned half-jokingly that she wanted to have ten children one day. Perhaps she was trying to run me off, but I am one of eight children, so I stayed.

It was providential meeting Krista when I did. Mr. Smith had just asked if I'd like to move two hours west to Clearwater, to work in the Tribune's bureau-by-the-beach. My answer was "Couldyourepeatthatplease?Yes." He handed me the horse-racing and Florida State League baseball beats. Later I was awarded the Tampa Bay Devil Rays beat. Somehow I had become a major league baseball writer.

It would be more than two years before Tampa Bay would even play its first major league game, but as I traveled to Charleston, South Carolina; Durham, North Carolina; and other Devil Rays minor-league affiliate towns to watch games and find stories, I considered more than once that my writing purgatory was probably worth it, for I had reached something that felt like, well, heaven. I was watching professional baseball, which I had done with sheer joy since I was a small child, and now I was even being paid for it.

I asked Krista to marry me during the spring training before the Devil Rays' inaugural major league game. She bought me a German Shepherd puppy. I named him Eddie. Yeah, so what of it?

I was living on a quiet pass, and I would come home from games around midnight and collapse on the hammock in my backyard. Because of the frenzy of deadlines, my hyperalert state never permitted immediate sleep. So I'd read from a book inches from the lapping waters of the Gulf of Mexico. And most of the time I'd just fall asleep out there.

We married right after the baseball season. Rich was my best man. Eddie Murray was the other. I'm joking about the second guy.

From our honeymoon in Italy, we agreed we didn't want a childproof first year of marriage, so we clinked glasses of Chianti on the extreme and graced hillsides of the Portofino coast and toasted our future bambinos. Life was light and so wonderful.

Married life was rolling along.

Then...poof.

DEBILITATING NEWS

I picked up the ringing phone one morning, and a doctor told me my sperm count was low and it was unlikely Krista and I would be able to conceive without medical intervention. I hung up the phone and stared at the bedroom wall for the time it takes to play two innings of baseball.

Eventually I went out and grabbed my bike and started pedaling past the waving palm trees of my Treasure Island neighborhood, wondering how to break the shotgun-blast news to Krista when she got home. Within minutes I passed two mothers walking their babies in strollers. Wonderful.

I pedaled away from my neighborhood and crossed two-lane Gulf Boulevard, imagining that a long walk on the beach could ease the emerging fire in my head. But small children splashed merrily there, and parents snapped pictures wildly, so I left, mental inferno fully ablaze. (A kind piece of advice for those who discover they're possibly infertile: Do not proceed to the beach within two hours of hearing the news.) Soon I discovered that, unless we wanted to start life anew in Greenland, all these adorable babies gooing and gaaing around every corner were going to pose an emotional dilemma for my wife and me.

When Krista and I managed to leave our weariness behind, we cared for each other as best we could, a wobbly model of a newly married couple balancing budding love with mounting sorrow. We consoled one another with compassionate talks on our back porch, which overlooked the quiet pass that pulled in the warm flow from the Gulf of Mexico. We strolled arm-in-arm on the moonlit beach, when babies were sleeping, and began to strategize on a future we couldn't quite agree upon. It seemed out there under the starlight that we were two grains of sand attempting to challenge a problem mightier than the sea.

We escaped for short weekend vacations when we felt the monster was gaining on our wounded psyches. But the respites never worked. St. Augustine's narrow cobblestone streets, Captiva Island's shell-stocked shoreline, and Tarpon Springs's Greek restaurants were momentary, flimsy fixes. We kept away from Orlando.

Throughout the early stages of our grief, our prayer life intensified, though it seemed as if we were praying underwater. Poor Krista made daily late-morning visits to St. John Vianney Church by the shoreline, where she served as youth minister. In cool silence she fell to her knees in front of a soft-smiling statue of the Blessed Mother off to the right of the altar. After thirty or so minutes of prayers, pleas, and promises, Krista would fold the kneeler, leave the church, and walk down a corridor to the lunchroom, where the seventh- and eighth-grade children she taught overwhelmed her with easy, innocent talk. I imagine Krista sort of smiling, listening to them gab as they shared Oreos with her. I can still envision my bride thanking them with tears welling—but not falling, I don't think.

Meantime I interviewed athletes, scribbled notes, banged out passionless stories, closed my laptop, and often wept.

Mornings I often prayed the rosary from our dock as wildlife burst all around like some giant outdoor jubilee. A nervy family of egrets accepted bread from my fingertips. Dolphins made daily sojourns, and Hail Marys were interrupted by mullets leaping into the sunshine. I watched sharp-toothed yellow jacks buzz the water and zebra-striped sheepshead doze lazily beside small rays in the shade beneath the dock. And like someone out of his head, I contrasted the booming nature that sprang to life each morning with my bad biology.

I, too, pleaded for the Virgin's intercession and light touch, though I figured that it likely wasn't going to arrive in the desired manner—with an endearing bump in my wife's midsection. My prayers of petition felt disordered and frenzied, probably not unlike the lunatic prayers Peter flung about the desert hours after rejecting his best friend.

While trying to place myself in the presence of Christ, I routinely took the flashing off-ramp into myself, crying out for a child I was all but certain wouldn't come. But as muddied and directionless as my prayer life was, it at least offered cheap succor for the pain. What else could I do? I needed communication with Christ, even if it was just to uncork all the mess inside.

When I wasn't in Christ's ear, I immaturely dialed up saints. St. Jude (long-shot miracle) and the Little Flower ("Please let a rose spring up from the sand"), and many of my other haloed favorites were hearing from me too often. I imagine they were throwing up their arms and berating me as kindly as a saint is able, with the only four words that essentially mean anything: "God's will, not yours." But if they were trying to reach me, I never heard a word.

I often attended weekday Mass and thanked God for my new bride, dream job, and good friends. But my wild-eyed will kept barging in and eviscerating things. Soon I was begging for his healing hand, the same hand he offered to the paralytic, Lazarus, Mary Magdalene, the demoniac, and all the others. I rationalized like a five-year-old: "You helped them, Christ. Why not me?" It wasn't difficult to notice that the recycled prayers for resolution were completely suffocating my relationship with God.

Ironically, for some time I had imagined my prayer life as an invisible umbilical cord stretching all the way to Christ in heaven. I used to envision a tiny dove rocketing down that long chute to alight on me with the love of Christ. When I was rich in prayer, a profusion of God's sustaining graces and peace was alive within me.

But my frenetic prayers for resolution cut the cord and managed to sabotage the very root of my being. Consequently my prayer life became spiritless. So the dove flew back to his perch, seemingly awaiting a more thoughtful version of myself.

FOOD FOR THE JOURNEY

Growing up, I'm certain there were many nights when my Dad brought constellations of concerns to our dining room table. After his father died from Lou Gehrig's disease, he was forced to lead a successful contracting business by himself. But as his pile of children gathered each night to dive into dinner, I don't remember sensing weariness.

Each morning Mom would spread half a loaf of Giant bread onto the kitchen counter for school lunches and not bat an eye as her butter knife made its initial descent into the Giant peanut butter jar. Her hair turned white watching us bring home boyfriends and girlfriends who made her flinch. She pulled Hardy Boys and baseball mitts out of bathtubs, watched us climb onto the roof-peak of our gray-blue colonial, and carpooled us to faraway baseball diamonds for games in towns we would never see again.

It's very likely Dad's and Mom's occasional groans were vocalized far from earshot, but I certainly wasn't aware. I was lucky enough to learn that obstacles and grief needed to be triumphed over, not dwelled upon. I'm certain that my parents' many confrontations with difficulties were attended by the shadowy confluence of doubt and faith. But they seemed to always tend toward the side of faith—never easy navigation for parents. And because I played witness to the solidarity of their approach, I was given an early blueprint on how to confront, and hopefully navigate past, life's little earthquakes.

Like birds building a thick winter's nest straw by straw, Mom and Dad fortified and insulated me with steady reminders of Christ's sacrifice on the cross, fully aware that I would encounter crosses of my own down the line. I didn't realize it then, but as my body lurched forward, tattoos of old-school Catholic relics were being burned into me with piecemeal precision to help equip me for those future struggles. Monthly confessions, novenas, Scripture readings, bedtime prayers, and dinner-table spirituality were the ubiquitous, reassuring rhythms that escorted me through my young, trouble-free life.

The unified front of my parents and the Sisters of St. Joseph, who taught me for eight years at St. Pius X School in my Bowie, Maryland, hometown, introduced me to Jesus Christ and the unbending solidity and splendor of my faith. I was taught that Christ was the guide who could enable a peace that the world simply could not provide. To acquire peace, I was taught how to pray. Mom and Dad told me a relationship with my Father simply could not occur without steadfast prayer. I've felt pulled to follow their teaching since I was strong enough to kneel against the wooden slats of my bottom bunk.

As a family we said rosaries in just about every room in our house, except the blue, pink, and yellow bathrooms. An assortment of rosary beads was kept in the glove box for car rides. Neighborhood friends, including some Protestants and at least one great Jewish friend, would pile into our station wagon for trips to baseball games and be invited to lead a decade of the rosary. I can still see Paul Schmidt's saucer eyes when it was his turn to lead the third sorrowful mystery. Andrew Kaufman, sitting alongside, wouldn't be much help.

During Lent I happily went to daily Mass and even attempted, and immediately failed, to give up teasing my sisters Chrissy and Karen. I began to fathom the splendid significance of the Stations of the Cross and hoped one day I would be as bold as Veronica and Simon the Cyrene. By age six I knew that the Eucharist was supposed to be the centerpiece of my life. Five minutes with warm-hearted, Irish-brogued Fr. Cassin in confession would leave me feeling like a miniature spiritual all-star. I couldn't wait to take the test to become an altar boy.

All the while I was beginning to grasp and value the mystery of sanctifying grace and the fact that Christ should be approached with a healthy combination of reverence, fear, and love. Although I knew I was supposed to be a good kid, I started to understand that it was only through his tender mercies that this could even begin to occur.

I had always understood that I was a dead man without his Spirit fully alive within me. However, all that didn't prevent my prayer life from dissolving into a pity party.

chapter four

Providential Night

As a newly married man, I wasn't doing very well. There is God's will. And I think there's a cocky tendency to want to trespass on it and customize it to fit our particular need. That was me. And that was my prayer life.

Krista and I began to research in vitro fertilization and almost immediately discovered that the Catholic Church forbade it. The revelation blindsided us, and our little lives were rocked again. And as the devil is wont to do, he seemed to analyze our unified brokenness and in serpentine fashion begin to stroke us in all the perfectly wrong places.

Prior to our marriage we lived in separate houses, agreed to postpone lovemaking until Italy, and worshipped and prayed together. We strengthened our spirituality on parish retreats, were active with outreaches, and openly and joyfully discussed how Christ was working in our lives. We agreed, perhaps simplemindedly, that I would become a priest should we split, and Krista would join an order of nuns. We viewed our Catholic faith as our unerring guidepost.

But the jarring news of how the Church views in vitro fertilization started a small fissure, which led to a widening crack. The Catholic Church stands alone as the only major faith to condemn the medical process, considering it a major manipulation of nature and a danger to viable embryos.

When the issue of how to begin our family reared its head—which was every day—we pleaded our cases and rarely found neutral ground. Krista was convinced an attempt at in vitro fertilization was justified because, remarkably, our pastor said it could be considered permissible. She had the arsenal she needed to further plead her case.

I was becoming increasingly convinced that our plight was God's will and that we probably shouldn't mess with it. I didn't, however, blame Krista for her fierceness, especially after our doctor assured us, per our request, that no embryos would be put at risk. In effect, we determined that the procedure—in the eyes of the Catholic Church—would be only "unnatural."

Soon I would be joining the Hatfield clan, and Krista the McCoy. The pictures from Italy were still stuffed in the shoe-box in our family room for guests to view.

One thing we did agree upon: We would consider adoption.

PACKING UP OUR SORROWS

We fled Florida in the early spring of 2000. Sunshine didn't feel that good anymore; it just added sweat. We agreed to move to my suburban hometown in Maryland, where we hoped my large family would serve up a healthy smothering of home-baked compassion and support. We packed the U-Haul at night and set off for perhaps the loneliest northbound I-95 trip ever taken.

After ten years of writing professionally for newspapers, I had quit. Krista had quit horses and her job as a youth minister. I was to become a supervisor for my father's three-generation masonry contracting company, one of the oldest surviving masonry outfits in the Washington, D.C., metropolitan area. Because I enjoyed writing, I had avoided joining the company after college. But now I needed the job, and I knew it would provide the financial means for a possible adoption.

Fortunately, the company was busy and growing. I dove in, building a bank account with bricks and mortar.

We continued to fight. (The issue was packed into the U-Haul with all the other stuff.) Krista wasn't actively pursuing adoption; she was researching local doctors who performed in vitro procedures. She wanted to feel a baby in her body; she'd cut off an arm to get at it. I wanted to research adoption agencies. There was no middle ground.

Above our small apartment Satan surveyed potential marital roadkill, and he circled like the blackest of vultures.

I was sitting in beltway traffic one day when I phoned my uncle, Msgr. Thomas Wells, desperate. I had postponed making the call for months. Tommy, as the world seemed to call him, was considered by many to be a small miracle as a priest. Literally thousands of people will tell you how his enormous warmth had a way of flowing directly into the coldest parts of their souls.

Among the many gifts at his disposal, he seemed to have mastered the art of finding the human condition. He came at people and their problems from a constellation of angles. If you were serious-minded, he'd summon wisdom. Have a sense of humor? He'd knock you to the floor with wit. Hate God? He'd hate why you hated him, then he'd bring you around. You'd walk into his presence crestfallen or ready to fight and go home wringing personality and cheer out of your clothes. And you'd smile that evening as you put your head on the pillow.

Because he loved his Catholic faith and its impenetrable truths, I knew Tommy would defend its teaching on in vitro fertilization. I had kept Krista away from him, but our anger and desperation were spiraling out of control. We were walking around our apartment like ticked-off zombies.

"Buddy, come over," Tommy said to me over the phone. "Bring Krista."

Krista, God bless her, was fully aware of the stance Tommy would take. She decided to go anyway. It would be two against one, but regardless, she chose to pick a fight with Tommy in order to stand up for the child she knew could grow within her womb. On our tense hour ride over to Germantown, I decided I had never loved Krista more.

WORDS OF HOPE

We parked the car and found Tommy waiting for us in the parking lot of Mother Seton Church, where he served as pastor. He lovingly threw his long arms around Krista and led us to the small wooden deck of his tiny rectory. He opened a bottle of cheap Merlot and mocked me for being his long-lost prodigal nephew. We settled into fold-out plaid deck chairs.

The colors of the dusk sky were changing. Soon so would our lives.

Tommy got right to work. In a manner we hadn't previously even considered, he explained that bearing our blue whale–sized cross was a privilege. He said that Christ was allowing us to participate in the carrying of his cross and that our suffering and surrender to his will were an act of love to him. He said offering up and handing over our anguish to God could be a perfect prayer because it would unite us to him.

He talked of hope—not today's notion of contrived "hope" that's bathed in fleeting grins and warm emotion but the hope that groans in a secret, disregarded silence. He talked of the hope that demands a spinal column and a whispered, "Yes, I will trust you," even when all is unknown, even when every cell in your body points you in the other direction.

A faithful surrender to God's puzzling plan of our infertility, he admitted, did seem hopelessly futile when presented with the conquering, tempting powers of science. But he also pointed out that acceptance of even the worst of crosses would lead to unanticipated, wonderful experiences of God's loving goodness. He suggested that we fully embrace our pain, present it at the foot of Christ's cross, and pray daily for a patient acceptance of his divine will. He promised that God had great things in store. The cross, he said, was the doorway to peace.

"Hard to understand, I know," he said with that smile of his. "But that goodness will be revealed."

As we listened to him, our strife began to melt. Peace? It was as if Tommy was designed for such moments, and that it would have been OK if time had stopped on his back deck to allow our scabs of cynicism to break apart and lift and float away into the summer sky. But it was time for us to move forward, to attempt to enter together into this silent groan.

As we left, Tommy stopped poor Krista on the walk to the car. "I'll be there for you," he said, hugging her beneath the night's first stars, "throughout it all."

Two days later, in that same rectory, he was murdered.

chapter five

Tommy

I still have a postcard he sent from Ireland that had one of those roadside donkeys on it. I flipped it over and read, "Kevin, I've never seen a better card to describe what I felt like after totaling a car here." That was Tommy.

He had shattered his kneecap and cracked some ribs after a dumb road maneuver on one of those narrow, western coast roads. "I'll survive," he continued on. "As every Irish person says [in brogue], 'These tings happen.'"

When Tommy danced at weddings or swung a golf club, his inelegance left some wondering if he had a skeletal disease. He blew up one of my dad's old station wagons in New Hampshire and knocked on our door the following night holding a Maryland license plate. "Here's your car," he said straight-faced.

Line up five hundred priests in a row, and he'd be voted funniest. Because of that humor an attractive woman in a Galway pub tried to pick him up while I watched. And for the first time in my life, I saw awkwardness dilute his bright blue eyes, then watched discomfort travel to all parts of his slender frame.

He had more friends than anyone I know. Perhaps as many as two hundred times a year he was invited to someone's home for dinner. Often, without asking, he'd stroll into the kitchen as if it were his own and sample the meal still being cooked. Later, around the table, he'd dispense Christ-centered guidance with the powered magnetism and elegance of Lombardi in a stadium's underbelly.

He told stories that brought tears of laughter, nostalgia, or even shame, depending on how the mood moved that evening. He'd pass the potatoes while laying a haymaker to a flat-footed, red-faced teen, asking questions in the open that others wouldn't dare in private. "So, pleeease tell me you and Marybeth aren't fooling around behind your parents' backs." As dinnerware was being cleared, he'd cuddle the baby and sing an Irish lullaby in a soft, lousy brogue.

The mind-boggling and marvelous aspect of his wide popularity was that he walked the world without a verbal straightjacket. Where other men ostracized themselves with a direct approach, Tommy could look a man in the eye and tell him he was on a path leading to hell. After some time of anger and reflection, that same man would end up in Tommy's golf foursome.

He had been taught the splendor of truth by wise spiritual guides at Christ the King Seminary in upstate New York, and he understood it would have been a crying, Milquetoast shame to bottle up that truth. Instead of lying in the weeds with the shifting sands of the culture, Tommy held nothing back; he knew a wholesale submission to the divine will was the only way. Christ came into the world to bear witness to the truth, and Tommy felt compelled to at least try and do the same.

"Yeah, it's harder than hell sometimes," he'd say to me in his way. "But ya gotta do it his way."

Hanging on walls throughout a multitude of homes in the D.C. area today is his favorite refrain stenciled within picture frames: "People! If I can just get you to live every day with God and for God, then you will know happiness, and you will be ready for whatever happens." He would have taken a sabbatical if he were allowed to crisscross the country and puff out the message as a skywriter. He was echoing the first-century words of James: "So submit yourselves to God. Resist the devil, and he will flee from you. Draw near to God, and he will draw near to you" (James 4:7–8).

Because he knew that our moral condition remained grave without Christ's message lighting our way, he blasted himself into the world to remind us of God's measureless mercy and of his promise of graces. In the process of sharing God's message, he developed into a first-rate architect and renovator of souls.

He once picked up a banjo-strapped hitchhiker on Interstate 71 in rural Ohio. The teenager, a Canadian who hadn't been inside a church in years, had intentions of becoming a bluegrass star at the Grand Ole Opry. So Tommy steered his car toward Kentucky, and the pair spent the next few hours discussing matters of faith.

Well, today this man is a philosopher with a master's in theology. He's a deacon and philosophy and religion instructor and former president of the Canadian

Fellowship of Catholic Scholars. "I became very aware of his joy," the hitchhiker said years later. "The joy I saw in his eyes was the living proof that what he was saying to me in that car was truth. I wanted what he had."

Because archdiocesan leaders understood they had a joyous, modern-day, pavement-beating fisher of men in their midst, they kept shipping Tommy to dying parishes. He obliged, lightheartedly hopscotching from all-black parish, to blue-collar parish, to affluent parish, to scandalized parish, to Spanish-speaking parish, and on and on. He moved around so much that he made return visits.

TOMMY TRADITIONS

We had traditions at Christmastime that had Tommy at the forefront. For twenty-some years he stood by the tree on Christmas night as comedian and master of ceremonies, calling out names and handing out gifts to the fifty-some of us squeezed into the living room. Thousands will tell you humor was his greatest gift. But it wasn't.

The night after Christmas Tommy treated those nieces and nephews who were old enough to a dinner feast. Somehow, throughout the course of those cozy nights, he managed, seamlessly, to make his way around the room to speak to each of us. Those nights were perfect. Thousands will tell you warmth was his greatest gift. But it wasn't.

Each Christmas Eve we watched him catch fire as he celebrated the Eucharist on the day when "the Word became flesh and made his dwelling among us" (John 1:14). Because he had a singular devotion to the Eucharist, his celebration of the Mass was vital in his life. He celebrated

every day of his twenty-nine years in the priesthood—
from altars, motel rooms, picnic tables, family rooms,
mountaintops. Wherever, whenever. Some will tell you
this was his greatest gift. And it was.

That was the heart of Tommy.

His friendships, his humor, his evangelization, and our
family traditions all met the guillotine on the night a
drug- and alcohol-fueled tree trimmer named Robert
Paul Lucas wedged himself through a small ground-floor
window with an aim to steal things. It's difficult to know
what happened that humid June night in 2000, when the
small Mother Seton rectory was transformed into a horror house.

When Tommy didn't post to celebrate Mass the following morning, a curious church employee entered the rectory and walked straight into the bloodshed. She found
Tommy with a drawer from his desk covering his head and
a multitude of stab wounds covering his body, like hell
stigmata. The palms of his hands were sheared by his
attempts to defend himself. Picturing Tommy in a fight was
like picturing Mother Teresa dunking a basketball.

The atmosphere of Washington, D.C., pivoted into a tangle of unruly emotions when the news report sprung from
Germantown that morning. A beloved area radio host
instantly changed his format and took call after call from
the stunned and brokenhearted. Sometimes an over-
wrought caller would have to stop mid-sentence, and all
that was audible was the crackle of airwaves.

As news of the violence was revealed in dribs and drabs
that day, souls were railroaded and flung into a country of

incoherence and horror. Whether the murdered priest was personally known or not, many drove home from work numb.

A TIDAL WAVE OF MOURNERS

A makeshift website launched by a parishioner of Mother Seton led to an e-mail from a man in Kilkenny, Ireland, which sprung a ten-thousand-strong inundation of farewell messages after only a few days. The myriad expressions of grief took the form of love letters, tributes, poems, and searing memories that did all but send tears running down the computer screen.

Car dealerships changed their marquees to say farewell. Steak dinners and beers were on the house for loved ones. Countless friends took sick days and zombied around from place to place. Newspapers and television broadcasts, which led daily with the latest news on the murder and the investigation, kept people fully engaged.

Waves of children, who loved Tommy in a manner that is hard to describe, hugged their mommies and cried on live television. Boy, did he love children. He'd enter classrooms and sing the Foundations' "Build Me Up, Buttercup" to loosen things up, then he'd yank one of his standbys from his back pocket—an old McDonald's jingle that he took liberties with:

McDonald's is your kind of place:
hamburgers in your face,
French fries up your nose,
dill pickles between your toes....
McDonald's is your kind of place.

At one Sunday Mass a small boy had summoned the courage to bring up the collection in a wicker basket, and Tommy had stooped down and looked the boy solemnly in the eye. "Did you take any of it?" he whispered in the boy's ear.

When I was a little kid, he'd visit my school to open up our eyes to God's special love for us. He'd always follow his talks with animated Q-and-A sessions, and if I was quiet that day, he'd announce gravely to the class, "I'm terribly sorry, students, but my nephew Keggy has come down with a severe case of laryngitis." Then in a flash he'd turn to my teacher, Sr. Edward, and whisper the words, "But God has richly blessed you with this illness, Sister."

Once he caught me sucking on my clip-on schoolboy tie and said, "Keggy, please. Lunch isn't for another hour." And the splendid explosion of children's laughter filled the St. Pius X classroom. That was Tommy.

Fire codes were broken at his funeral. Roads were shut down and traffic redirected as thousands poured in to say good-bye at Sacred Heart Church in Bowie, Maryland, where he started his ministry in the 1970s. A six-year-old girl wore her ivory-white First Communion dress for the first time that day. Later that night, as her mother tucked her into bed, the little girl looked into her mother's eyes and said, "I wish I could live closer to [Msgr. Wells's gravesite], so that every morning when I wake up, I can pray there."

Two hundred and fifty solemn-faced priests and deacons choked the vestibule prior to the funeral, as mourners were stacked six deep against the back and side walls of the church. Hidden among the hordes were seven young men well into the formation process that would lead them to the priesthood. Around these parts they call these seven men "the Wells guys," because Tommy was the spiritual catalyst who helped shepherd each to his vocation. "I owe him my life," said fresh-faced seminarian Greg Shaffer that day. More vocations would come.

Tommy's greatest friend, Fr. James Stack—Tommy called him "Stackman"—opened his homily with these words: "My friend Thomas Wells—mentor, advisor, golf buddy, traveling companion—has gone home to God. So I rejoice...." But his chin went soft, and his words were betrayed. And many mourners fell apart.

I had been chosen as lector for the first reading, a mournful passage from the book of Lamentations. But even as I mouthed the old words of Jeremiah, "The favors of the Lord are not exhausted" (Lamentations 3:22), only one record spun in my head: Krista had lost her newfound shepherd.

GIFT OF GARRYKENNEDY

I first told Tommy about Krista in a small pub along the banks of the Shannon River. We were in one of Ireland's tiniest riverside villages, Garrykennedy. It was one of those nights when I wished I could crush every clock in the house to lasso time.

Tommy had rented a giant farmhouse in the small country town of Portroe in County Tipperary, and he dispatched an invitation for family to visit him in the heart of Ireland. So fifteen or so of us gathered at the old house, which was hedged in by the Shannon and endless wavy acres of grassy farmland. Days filled with leisurely travel and promenades in the meadows were followed by evenings charged with storytelling, the kind that awakened the cows and would have made Yeats happy.

For a three-day span at the end of the rental period, Tommy and I had the farmhouse to ourselves. And things got even better.

A one-lane road led from the farmhouse to the charming village of Garrykennedy, which offered up two riverbank pubs like jackpot-winning lottery tickets. These were authentic Irish pubs, places where a visiting musician's lame go at "Danny Boy" would have gotten him thrown into the Shannon with a full keg tied to his neck. These candlelit places had magic within their walls— where part of the musical entertainment was a white-haired widow easing from a mahogany bench to resurrect an emigration song in the old language. This was the authentic "craic," as Tommy would often say, in which timeless traditions unfolded with an intermingling of mysticism and sacredness.

Since it was a comfortable evening, Tommy and I decided to walk down to Garrykennedy. We passed a smattering of farmhouses that were far off the road, wide fields choked with ruby-red corn poppies, thick hedgerows, and meandering stone "penny fences" that knifed through open bog lands and sun-drenched pastures. The summery hum of insects and grunts and groans of heifers and sheep followed us, along with the soft river breeze, as we laughed and laughed about a night in Ireland a few years earlier when the honey-sweet mead was poured too liberally at Bunratty Castle. Townsfolk who passed by in slow-moving cars so as to not kick up dust lifted index fingers briefly off their steering wheels, the old Celtic way of saying, "Good evening, and God bless."

We had worked up a thirst after our thirty-minute walk, and the bartender was serving Guinness. We seemed to be trailing the locals in the pint count, so we attempted to catch up at a table in the corner.

Tommy was immediately in his element, like Mickey Mantle when he stepped past the white threshold of a batter's box. Ireland had my uncle's heart, and its people helped it beat. He always said it was its people that made Ireland the emerald it is.

As with our earlier two-week trip to Ireland's western coast, I noted Tommy's absurd transition to the brogue, which had occurred mere hours after his plane taxied up to Shannon Airport's tiny terminal. "Ahh, hello dare, sir. Fer sure, you can join us for the Guinness. 'Onest, be a shame if ya din't."

"Tommy, you're doing it again."

"Ahh, Keggy, give the good Fahder a break now, won't ya?"

STARLIGHT BENEDICTION

"Tommy, I think I found a good one," I told him.

"Tell me."

"Well, her name's Krista, and she's Italian and Irish and beautiful. She loves riding horses more than anything in the world. She's quiet. And she doesn't remind me of any of the others."

"Keggy, that's probably a good thing."

"Thanks, Father.… What I mean to say is, she has a good heart. That's what I know for sure. And that she loves me.… She reminds me of Mom."

"Really?"

"Well, she doesn't care about all the stuff out there, like Mom doesn't, you know. She keeps it simple and appreciates the essential things. She loves children and loves God. You should see the way she works with the kids she's teaching riding lessons to."

"Sounds like the right one.… Do you love her?"

"Yeah, I think so."

"Well, then, if you think God has brought Krista to you, then I couldn't be happier for you."

I remember the Shannon breeze that flitted through the dark pub's open door that night and the Gaelic ballads dug from the souls of fishermen, farmers, and old widows. I remember how Tommy struck up conversations with humble-hearted locals whose sun-shot cheeks bore splotchy blue capillaries that rambled like Irish roadmaps. He inadvertently mentioned to some that he was a Catholic priest, and suddenly the table spilled over with fresh pints.

As we walked back to the farmhouse beneath a thick covering of twinkling starlight, the smoked-earth smell of peat hung in the soft Shannon air like Irish incense. And the night seemed like a benediction to the wholesomeness of old-country ways. Christ felt so close, like he was tucked in with us between the rushes and hedgerows.

Tommy witnessed our marriage a little over a year later.

"I'll be there for you," he told Krista at the end, "throughout it all."

I have thought of his words many, many times.

chapter six

Forward at a Crawl

They found his murderer ten days later in textbook lodging for a cold-blooded killer: an outdated brown-and-beige van hidden in a metallic forest of other dilapidated vehicles, tucked away on a country road. It was his boot print that betrayed him. Then it was the church property recovered from the back of the van.

The *Washington Post's* booming front-page story the following morning included a mug shot of Lucas that has lingered like a weed in the part of my mind that tries to bury things. He looked to be in the midst of a whiskey bender: His dark hair was wild; his eyes, aligned asymmetrically on his face, were set in a flat stare. He had a cleft lip and a country mustache. His shirt was pulled to the right, as if a cop had just grabbed a fistful of it to position him for the shot.

"He's sorry. He asked me to ask everyone to forgive him," his mother told a *Post* reporter. "He's having a hard time. He said he didn't know. He didn't even know where he was."

But deputy state attorney Kate Winfree batted down the statement within a second or two of its leaving the mother's mouth. Winfree explained to a beehive of reporters that Lucas had already provided a mountain of details about his arrival at the rectory, the crime, and his departure. "He knew [what he was doing] throughout the course of the night," Winfree said matter-of-factly.[1]

So Lucas became suicidal. He requested rope.[2]

Some say Tommy's murderer had been born into a life of nevers. He never was healthy—and almost died at two months. He never had many friends—he was routinely mocked by schoolmates. He never had a loving father—his treated him like a disease.

Some people even felt sorry for him. Some.

So we limped forward, grudgingly relocating Tommy into the cold repository of our memories.

Meanwhile the elements of a second nightmare were taking shape. The murder of a popular priest was just B-side stuff. In due time Satan, it seemed, was intent on unleashing a masterpiece.

Last Letter

As plans were in the works to bulldoze the rectory, Krista and I moved forward, carrying our invisible anchor of infertility in a Tommy-less world. Miraculously, though, we were given a mighty and providential wind to help us step together into our crucible. Three days after his death, Tommy managed to speak to us from the grave.

Many mourners scratched their heads when they read his final pastor's column in the June 11 issue of the Mother

Seton parish bulletin. Apparently he had penned the piece on his last day and sent it off to the parish secretary. The thousands of people who were looking for one last, consoling message in their time of grief were instead offered a column on the cross of infertility.

While others whispered, "Huh?" in puzzled disappointment, Krista and I wept. It was his love letter to us. Better, it was our roadmap.

"I'll be there for you throughout it all," he had promised my wounded bride. I wondered about the dimension and reach of those final words.

Within a day our Hatfield-and-McCoy quarrel had softened and finally run its course. Shotgun shells and mountaintop irritability gave way to a tender solidarity and stillness. In the wake of Tommy's death, we now knew our path. We agreed we would adopt a child.

For months Krista had approached in vitro fertilization with the tenacity and passion of her wild horse rides in her Florida meadow. But that old racetrack thoroughbred wouldn't give this time, and her dream to bring life into her womb was put down.

It is impossible to suitably describe the bottomless pain of infertility, especially for people like Krista and me, who had such a strong desire to bring life into the world. At the time though, I attempted to put my thoughts into words:

> Sweet child whom I will never see,
> I am sorry for keeping you from your world.
> I have buried you in the sorrowful casket that is my soul.

Nobody mourns your loss. No one thinks of you.

You would have loved your small house with its
big climbing trees.
You would have explored our fields and made
friends with deer.
I would have watched you from your bedroom
window
while you played catch with a friend.

I listen to the chorus of summer locusts and cry
now because you aren't beside me.
You will never hear these melodious summery
sounds.
You are on the other side somewhere, so far from
my embrace.
Boy, you were my shining dream.
Now you are my ghost.

I wrote this on August 27, 2000, beneath the longest branch of an enormous oak tree in the sprawling backyard of our tiny country home, which my UPS man called "The Gingerbread House." I couldn't have known it, but it was around this time that a sperm and egg united twenty-five miles down the road. A new life was firing forward. God was at work, helping to turn sad poetry into stunning and wonderful verse.

We attacked the paperwork and our home studies and endured the background checks, medical checkups, fingerprinting, and all the rest that go along with the adoption preliminaries. We made a scrapbook for birth parents, with loads of photos and letters from nieces and nephews and brothers and sisters. Johnny, the youngest of my parents' eight, wrote that I would be a good dad once the kid got over the teasing. So we waited on God for the child he had in mind for us.

NEW BEGINNING

A spunky young woman had been introduced to a handsome young man that summer, and a romance had ensued. The man took her virginity, and a baby was soon growing within her womb. That posed a problem: The man didn't want one there. He wanted his problem fixed with an abortion.

The young woman fought and pleaded for their child, but the father remained fixed. He behaved like a wounded wolf in his ferocity to have his way. Verbal abuse gave way to physical abuse, and after approximately three months of carrying her child, the young woman agreed to visit an abortion clinic with the one-way man.

Gabrielle Maria Wells is a smiler. She's the kind of child you see smiling by the apple stand in the grocery store. Ten minutes later she's smiling at you in Aisle 4 while helping Krista calm Shannon in the back of the shopping cart. "Oh, it's OK, Boo Boo. Mommy's almost finished." At the checkout counter she'll have a cantaloupe-slice smile as she helps load groceries into the cart. Gabby's smile is perhaps her greatest ornament.

If fetuses can smile, it wasn't the appropriate time when a Latina nurse approached the woman to wheel her into the back room. The emotionless man sat coolly beside her, content that events were finally unfolding his way. But sometimes magic and miracle merge, and firmly laid plans split and shed like onion peels in order to find another way.

Though the man was well educated, he could not understand Spanish. So after squaring her shoulders to her fear, the young woman looked the nurse in the eye and spoke in the nurse's native language: "When it is my turn, wheel me back into the room, but don't dare put a finger on my baby."

The obliging nurse assured her of her baby's safe passage, never once making eye contact with the unknowing man listening in on the conversation. So he continued to recline in his chair like a pillar of contentment, aware only that an abortionist stood in the back room.

Another day at the clinic. But this one turned.

An hour later the young woman was wheeled from the back room. She had wisely requested a sedative to make her appear groggy as she faced her man. He wore a sympathetic smile when their eyes met. Quickly it faded as the woman said, "Your child is dead. Now you are dead to me."

He drove home alone. She took the bus. And if fetuses can smile, Gabby did.

Four months after the non-abortion, Krista came down to the basement. It was Valentine's night. I was unromantically watching coverage of the Orioles pitchers and catchers, who had reported for spring training in Fort Lauderdale, Florida.

"Well, we got some news today," Krista said as I watched an easygoing gathering of young men in orange shirts embroidered with black numbers pile into an out-dated baseball clubhouse. Krista had bought a bottle of Chianti and some delicious takeout from a nearby Italian restaurant.

"Our agency called. We were chosen," she said with a flutter of hesitancy.

"Boy.... Uh, well?"

"A young woman saw our scrapbook and told the agency that she had found her daughter's parents. She's seven months pregnant and is doing great. She chose us, Kevin."

"Man.... What about the guy?"

"Gone. Out of the picture."

We sat nervously on the couch and peeled the foil from our Shrimp Fra Diablo and Calamari Fritte with lemon wedges and a heaping side of extra-spicy marinara sauce. I uncorked our honeymoon wine. "Happy Valentine's Day," I said.

"Happy Valentine's Day," said Krista.

"We're gonna be a family, huh?"

"Yeah. It looks that way."

Then we hugged—with a lot of hesitancy but even more hope, I think.

LOVE SWEEPS IN

The man wasn't the wiser when Gabby hurtled into the world a month early on a rainy night. I scissor-cut the umbilical cord and patted the sweet woman's forehead with a cold towel, as my wife spilled tears onto the face of her first child. Our hero handed Gabrielle to Krista and whispered in her honeyed accent, "Here, Kreesta. She's yours."

Three times now I've witnessed swollen-eyed women placing their child into my wife's arms for the last time. And each time their mind-bending act of selfless love and surrender has taken me to the foot of the cross. Like the marveling Roman centurion who was changed forever by the heroism that unfolded before him, I have been awed by these women, who've offered me glimpses of majestic, sacrificial love.

I know that at the moment of final placement—when the baby is bundled up and set to leave the hospital—the pools of sorrow in these women are as deep as the ocean floor. But thank God, they also seem to have a measureless reservoir of trust and sacrificial love to tap into. Perhaps these grieving women are aware that Christ is right there with them, shedding the same tear, softening the despair, and fortifying their stunning surrender to blind hope. I don't know. The glorious secret of their strength will forever be buried in their bloodstream.

Gabby's birth mother, who listened to classical music, salsa, and Bon Jovi with equal fervor, was whispering a Spanish lullaby to her baby when I cracked her door an hour before we were set to leave the hospital. She was spending her last hour with Gabrielle, cradling her and crying onto her tiny cheeks. She actually smiled through her tears when she saw me. "Oh, Kayveen," she said, "I used to sing this song to Gabby when I was pregnant. I knew it would help make her a happy girl."

She invited Krista and me into her room, where we hugged in silence for a long, long time.

Seemingly on the heels of Gabby came Sean, almost like her Irish twin. A wonderful, athletic young lady knew my large extended family and heard about our desire to adopt. She called us one night and asked if we would like to be the parents of her child. We met her and her mother a few days later at a nearby restaurant. They both told us that Tommy was the bond that had brought this unique union together.

"Oh, I can hear Tommy laughing out loud right now," the young woman's mother said from the Formica table. "I can see those happy blue eyes looking down with so much joy."

The reach?

Satan's Flight

In the cocoon of our infertility, we had moved to historic downtown Ellicott City, Maryland, a quiet town set deep into a gorge of steep, rocky hillsides. It was an old mill town and railroad stop that had managed to retain its appearance of a century earlier. We went to the Catholic church where Babe Ruth married his wife, Claire Mae, in 1929. We often joined the slow-paced rhythm of folks walking the hilly Main Street, which showcased unique antique stores, restaurants, and taverns.

But after Gabby was born, we peeled rubber to get out of the antique town and back into the welcoming arms of my family. I imagine a significant part of Krista still felt hollowed-out and far-flung from the many glowing female relatives and friends who were producing waves of babies around that time. But she tempered her emotions with graceful submission and an effective technique: She gazed at her growing daughter.

Sean joined us shortly thereafter at our brand-new home in Crofton, just down the street from the families of my brother Dan and sister Chrissy. The jigsaw puzzle was snapping together. Life took on a more pleasant rhythm, like the slumping batter who managed to resurrect his old swing. We met new friends and reunited with old ones. I was learning my new job, and Krista was loving hers too, as a beaming, full-time mom. She glowed.

My cell phone would ring from a job site in a ruinous part of Washington, D.C.

"Hi, Daddy," Krista would say. "Somebody wants to say hello." Silence.

"There. That was Gabby. She just wanted to tell you that she loves you."

"'Kay, honey, see you for dinner."

Life felt pretty good, as perfect as it could be, in fact.

We couldn't have known the magnitude of evil that was to befall us. No one could have. It was unimaginable.

CHANGE OF STRATEGY

Many months after the murder, word leaked from the state attorney's office that Lucas's defense attorneys were formulating a fundamental shift in strategy to help chisel away time for their client. Lucas's lawyers would soon claim that Tommy had attacked their client in the midst of the robbery at the Mother Seton rectory that night. They would say Tommy was not murdered in a fearful defense of his life but only after a passionate advance toward their client.

Lucas's defense attorneys would go on to claim that Tommy had repeatedly tried to seduce his killer that night and that Lucas was merely attempting to defend himself from his advances when he went for his knife. Lucas now "remembered" finding Tommy on top of him as he came to from his drunken stupor.

The big, red-brick courthouse in Rockville, Maryland, became the stage for a maelstrom—a chilling, bucking-bronco ride of a trial witnessed by incalculable numbers of people due to the descent of local television stations and big newspapers. Perhaps even the media couldn't comprehend the evil that penetrated the wood-paneled courtroom. Within minutes of the defense team's opening statement, some who loved Tommy headed for the exits. Friends shouted out in horror. The judge warned against such emotional outbursts; he would have to keep doing so.

As the trial pushed forward, Lucas's lawyers urged him to take the stand and tell his story in his own defense. He tried the best he could. He recalled leaving his favorite bar, the Magic Cue, a hard, honky-tonk beer hole a quarter mile down the road from the Mother Seton rectory. He subsequently urinated on himself and passed out in front of some bushes by the rectory. Upon waking up, he admitted, he broke into the rectory with the intent of "cleaning up."

Lucas said he was surprised when he was greeted by my uncle, who he claimed was in an amorous mood. Lucas said he again passed out, and when he awakened he found Tommy on top of him. He said that when he tried to escape, my uncle jumped on his back. It was only then that Lucas pulled out his folding knife.

"I had a knack for being able to just whip [the knife] with my wrist, and the blade would just fly open," he told the courtroom.[1]

Cross-examination came rather hard for Lucas, as Kate Winfree and dashing state attorney Doug Ganzler bore wide holes in his story. Lucas kept looking with uncertainty toward his lawyers, and he often stammered. He admitted he had radically altered his original account of what happened the night of the murder. He said he couldn't recall how he ended up with so many rectory items in his van.

"You have a lot of memory problems, don't you, Mr. Lucas?" Winfree asked.[2]

"Some might say that," he said in a puny voice.

RESOLUTE PRAYER

During recesses countless members of Tommy's family and friends stood sentinel outside the courtroom, praying the rosary in a wide, meandering circle. It was a strange landscape, where breathing space was shared with the much smaller Lucas family. A courtroom artist drew a touching portrait of Lucas's mother joining us in a rosary one day. Many in our prayer circle believed Tommy was forgiving his murderer right until the final thrust of Lucas's knife, so we became resolved to try to do the same.

The chilling nature of the trial made me want to dive into a Peanuts comic strip and lie noiselessly beside Snoopy to watch the clouds roll by. I think each of Tommy's backers at times wanted to hibernate. But we all seemed to know that unwavering prayer would be the only route to take. We continually gravitated toward it, to assuage our helplessness and to submit ourselves fully to God.

The lies Lucas unfurled often left us dizzy, but none of it

knocked us from our feet. He just seemed like a well-coached pawn. The anger I harbored wasn't directed toward Lucas but toward his well-coiffed attorneys.

One was a youngish-looking lady who throughout the trial couldn't seem to shake her gawkish air. The male attorney, who sported a tight column of gel-drenched hair, glided around the courthouse grounds in shiny suits, seemingly without a care for what he said. He'd chat with colleagues in corridors and smile with extraordinary ease. The bright eyes of the television cameras were set right on the two attorneys, and they seemed to flourish under its heat.

It was Satan, though, who seemed to be the most active participant in the courtroom.

What the devil hadn't considered, perhaps, was the scale of the fight he had picked: he was waging his war for disorder against a consolidated front of forgiveness and hope. He could not win.

The venue was full of Tommy's many friends and family members, who were quietly begging their God to lay his finger upon them. We implored Christ to help us persevere past the horrors, to lift our distressed souls and place them above and beyond all that was unfolding within the courtroom. We knew Christ understood our suffering, so we placed all of our anguish in his hands. And that seemed good enough.

Instead of picking fistfights with Lucas's family members in hallways or lashing out in front of television cameras, Tommy's supporters stood poised and undaunted. We continued to thumb our rosaries and contemplate the sacred rhythms of the mysteries in a soothing, audible oneness outside the courtroom. Newsmen, curious onlookers, and members of the Lucas family often just stared and tried to keep quiet.

Instead of yielding to cynicism before reporters' microphones, we spoke constantly of forgiveness. *Washington Post* reporters transcribed our quotes correctly, and tens of thousands of readers could ponder them if they chose.

And the best part of it—we looked kind of normal. We didn't resemble some form of burnt-out Branch-Davidian cult. We were just doing what we thought Tommy would have us do.

Satan was losing.

Then he lost. A jury of seven men and five women came out of sequester late one afternoon, two weeks after the trial began, to say that Lucas had lied. Guilty, they said.

For two weeks in that courtroom, I had been introduced to a scale of evil that I hadn't known existed. It was about to be matched.

chapter eight

Christ in the Moon

As a child, most nights I would lie in bed and whisper prayers in the direction of the bunk above. Thrown in at the end was an odd plea to God that my mom suggested I include. I prayed I would marry a loving wife who would bless us with children. Imagine that. A kid praying for a kid one day.

State Road 37 is a thin vein that runs past deep phosphate pits in scrubland Florida. The lonely stretch of road shoots past mossy oak hammocks, pines, open fields, and abandoned cabins while hurtling toward outposts you've never heard of—Bowling Green, Duette, Fort Lonesome. It's the quiet boulevard of farmers, migrant workers, and quarrymen. The road dies at a dot town called Keentown at the intersection of State Road 62. If you were there now, no one would be nearby.

But SR 62 was a road I came to love after moving to Florida. It was lonelier than heartbreak and quieter than midnight at Bethlehem but a perfect escort. It was SR 62 that freed me from Winter Haven's suffocating limits and led me to the resplendent white sands and lightly lapping shorelines of Sarasota and Bradenton. I'd just aim my old Toyota down the lonely road, roll down my windows, uncork the Waterboys' "Fisherman's Blues" to full radio volume, and dream the only dream I had at the time: to become a major league baseball writer. It was a happy time out on SR 62.

Today I shudder when I think of that road. SR 62 eventually betrayed me. She led me to a nightmare.

BLUE EYES, LIKE YOURS

One summer day a young man we'll call Ron told me that my newborn son was waiting for me at a medical center on the west coast of Florida. "Kevin, you're not gonna believe this," stocky Ron said over the phone. "He even looks like you. He's got blue eyes and all."

"Come on over. We're in Room 407."

Eight months earlier Ron and his girlfriend—we'll call her Karen—had asked us to be the parents of their child. It had been a very long eight months. Rambling late-night phone calls that awakened Gabby and Sean, missed appointments, shameless money requests, and unremitting erratic behavior marked their time with us. Living in Maryland and adopting in Florida is like trying to hit a knuckleball drunk.

But because Karen had a child growing within her womb, her cranky voice reigned sovereign. She repeatedly wanted to meet with us. A week didn't pass when she or Ron didn't complain about their treatment from our adoption agency. After one series of fitful phone calls concerning supposed unmet demands from our agency,

Krista hopped in our car and drove through the night to Florida's west coast. Seventeen hours.

"I thought you were going to be here earlier," Karen, eyelids pinched, said to Krista.

"I'm sorry," Krista said.

Our adoption agency felt that although Ron and Karen were often unpredictable and irritable, they seemed determined to follow through on what could seem like a shipwrecked adoption plan. So we tiptoed through our eight-month landscape of land mines, finding an oasis of calm only when we considered where the path might eventually lead us.

Now John Paul was born.

Ron's phone call sent Krista and me into a shock of joy, like the feeling in early springtime when as a boy I was finally able to shed my jacket to play baseball. In anticipation of his birth, we were staying at Krista's parents' house, a two-hour drive from the hospital. We quickly packed an overnight bag, received congratulatory hugs, and bolted for my old friend, SR 62, where I aimed the car toward our blue-eyed baby boy in Room 407.

When I pulled into the hospital parking lot, I noticed that much of the ocean of blacktop seemed to have just been poured. A large portion of the lot didn't even have the paint to indicate parking spaces. There aren't enough cars here, I thought. Where are the people who should be milling around? Then I noticed something else, which I hoped Krista hadn't. There were only three floors.

We tried the first door we saw, but it was dead-bolted. We saw a smaller entrance in the distance and hurried toward it. It was open. We walked in but were greeted by noiselessness. There was no receptionist behind the counter. No orderlies. No patients shuffling around.

I recall thinking that I knew the hospital had recently opened and that we were probably in the wrong wing. But I also knew that we had circled the hospital twice before pulling our car into a random spot on the steaming asphalt. We walked empty hallways for three minutes; then I noticed that Krista had been rendered wordless.

After some time we heard women's voices. We cut a path for the conversation and eventually found a small station where three nurses were gathered around a computer screen. We stopped in front of them. One nurse looked up.

"We're looking for room 407," I said, rushed, "and a baby born this morning."

"No, I think you may have something mixed up, sir," the nurse said.

"No, I'm not mixed up. We were told our friend Karen had a baby boy and is in Room 407 right now."

"Sir, we don't have our obstetrics or maternity ward set up yet," the nurse said. "And we don't have a fourth floor."

SCAMMED

The other two nurses stopped what they were doing to study us. Then they looked to my wife's right arm, in which she held an empty baby carrier. We had been scammed; we immediately knew.

I grabbed Krista's free hand and pirouetted her back in the direction from which we'd come. I scanned walls for exit signs, as our labyrinthine journey had disoriented us.

Krista was in a different country now, and I knew I wouldn't be able to reach her anytime soon.

When we were finally able to break back into the sun-baked afternoon, we moved past waving palm trees toward the open sea of asphalt, feeling as if we had been jerked into a late stage of the dying process. I threw the baby carrier into the back seat, then decided to cover it carefully with John Paul's powder blue blanket.

"Nothing I know of has ever happened on the scale of what happened to you," the program director for our agency later told us. "Not on *Dateline,* not on any news shows. Not in my twenty years of doing this."

For eight months we had happily provided for Karen's rent, food, doctor's visits, counseling sessions, maternity clothing, cell phone minutes, and more. We were the steel rod of financial support for the straw-haired woman who had a baby—or was the baby still in her womb?—now likely to be hawked on the black market. The thought was mind-blowing.

But as I pulled onto the interstate, my mind was on the broken flower who sat inconsolably next to me.

I didn't know where to go. After driving aimlessly for a while, I decided on a small shoreside motel that Krista and I liked. There I threw our suitcase and John Paul's bag of baby stuff into the room and hurried us off to an outdoor restaurant that looked dead into the sun, which was dropping into the flat, dark Gulf of Mexico.

In the wake of this magnificent evil, I didn't know how to properly comfort Krista. Tenderness wouldn't cut it. So I just sat close and stared with her into the darkening sea as a tidal breeze did its best to oblige us. And for a long while the torturous backdrop twang of a Jimmy Buffet sound-alike was the only noise that cracked the silence as we stared into a sky shot with red.

A short while later the bartender asked how I was doing. I'm not the type who chats it up with bartenders, but I needed to hear a voice. "I'm in the midst of what seems to be a nightmare," I said as I watched the lengthening shadows veil Krista at our table in the sand.

He asked why, and I told him. When we received our check for dinner and drinks three hours later, the bill came to $5.51. "To new beginnings," he had written at the bottom of the tab.

Moving On

There's a point where you don't care about the architect of the wickedness. I was just trying to stay ahead of the darkness.

It was a week later, and Krista was still disconsolate. I had removed John Paul from our insurance policy, taken down his in utero photo from our refrigerator, and navigated through the perilous waters of explanation to Gabby and Sean. We were extremely busy at work, and I was rolling around the Washington, D.C., metropolitan area in a seething anger. I told the compassionate collection of stunned family and friends at the time that I didn't want to talk about it. It wasn't the large amount of scammed money that bothered me; it was the loss of our boy, the horrific conclusion, and what the scam did to my wife.

The scale of the evil cut into my relationship with Christ. Why in the world, God? I mean, what are you thinking, Man? Have you taken inventory of my wife lately?

One day I saw an item in the bulletin from our parish, Our Lady of the Fields. The church needed volunteers for a weekly hour of Eucharistic Adoration. I called the parish secretary, told her to anchor me in for the 7–8 PM slot, and promised I would never be late. She didn't know that the volunteer on the phone had signed up not to adore but to excoriate. It had never been like this before.

Thirty years earlier the awesome significance of the Eucharist had been indelibly stamped into my life. Probably because my classmate Holly and I were loud-mouthed kids, we were chosen as lectors for a bimonthly school Mass at St. Pius X School. And because we were willing participants in the celebration of the Mass, we were afforded luxury seats at the altar, close to the celebrant, Fr. Charlie.

None of our seventy-or-so second-grade classmates had made their First Communion—and neither had Holly and I. However, that didn't stop Fr. Charlie from solemnly walking toward us at Communion time with the Host in his fingertips. That was an oversight.

He stopped like a six-foot boulder in front of me, stooped down, and said four words that had never been spoken to me before: "The Body of Christ." Not knowing what to do, I mumbled something, opened my mouth as wide as a three-day-old robin, and received my first Holy Communion—not only a year too soon but while my mom was at home washing the dishes.

Fifteen minutes later Mom wasn't washing dishes any-more. She was speeding down Belair Drive to my school, to meet with her confused son in the principal's office.

I remember thinking with Holly that something odd had just taken place—but we couldn't quite put a finger on it. We knew we shouldn't have accepted the Host, but we fig-ured, immaturely, that it may have been a royal perk for those fortunate to be seated like kings and queens at the altar. Plus, we weren't about to turn down Fr. Charlie. You could probably go to hell for that.

Immediately after Mass we were approached by both of the second-grade teachers and rushed down to meet with our principal, Sr. Jane. Parents were called. Fr. Charlie was informed of his unfortunate error. Holly and I were hemmed in by a small forest of frowning elders in the prin-cipal's office.

We were in big trouble. Jesus had come too soon.

POWERFUL REALITIES

My second-grade mistake came with a jarring but unfor-gettably beautiful realization: This precious centerpiece of my Catholic faith—the Eucharist—should never be taken lightly. I realized then—enveloped by anxious adults—that shattering a windowpane with an errant baseball throw, hiding broccoli in Karen's ice cream, or refusing to empty the trashcans in the blue, yellow, and pink bathrooms belonged in an entirely different category than did accept-ing the Eucharist before it was my time. Although I couldn't comprehend it then, the basic underpinnings of my devotion to the Holy Eucharist were laid that day.

Today I can't imagine my life without Jesus Christ as its marrow. How wonderful that our faith has bequeathed to us so many gifts—the sacraments, Scripture groups, retreats, spiritual guidance, outreaches, schooling, friends, bull and oyster roasts, and the like. But all of it would be rendered virtually meaningless without the marvelous miracle of Christ present in the Eucharist.

When Jesus dined with the twelve the night before his death, he altered the typical Passover meal and made himself the focus. He broke some bread, gave it to his friends, and said, "This is my body, which will be given for you; do this in memory of me" (Luke 22:19).

The powerful reality of our faith is that our Church has not wavered in its belief that Christ shares his love and life with us through this Blessed Sacrament. In an unbelievably intimate and loving way, Christ chooses to give himself freely to us regardless of our condition. We can approach Christ at Communion weakened, saddened, fatigued, confused, or—tragically—bored, but because our Savior loves us so much, he chooses to give freely of himself no matter what our response.

And that's the daunting part of the Eucharistic equation: At Communion we can accept the real presence without ourselves being "really present." But isn't it just like Christ to take that chance with us? He offers himself in this sacred banquet regardless of our condition, though as a maturing Catholic, I know I should consider the sacredness of the exchange and receive him only when I am without mortal sin and in a state of grace.

Holly and I were wide-eyed, silly kids. We should have kept our mouths shut. But the fact is, something momentous took root in me that day. Christ became part of me in a radical, giving, real way. He did for Holly, too.

However, in the aftermath of our adoption nightmare, I went on strike from proper veneration of Christ's renewing, hidden-in-a-Host presence. I was locked in on the magnitude of the evil and its bizarre finish.

When I mentally took down the scaffolding behind the scam, I saw where I could have handled things far differently. I could have kept in better contact with the adoption agency and cut things off after the first few distress signals. I could have paid closer attention to the telltale signs of a possible scam. Often throughout our tortured path to John Paul, my instincts told me the couple was suspect at best, but I kept buying into their lies—hoping perseverance alone would manage to overcome their truckload of deceit. I should have been begging God for wisdom and discernment at that time. I should have surrendered John Paul to God and asked that he fulfill his plans in a different and perhaps better way.

But like the beaten boxer with blood-stained trunks who continues climbing from his stool to face his smiling foe in the late rounds, I made the decision for Krista and me to keep stepping into Ron and Karen's eight-month flurry of uppercuts. We wobbled forward to the very end, when the pair threw one last blow.

SIXTY MINUTES

I dragged my backpack of grief and anger into Adoration, where I stared at the Host, which stared back at me like a fairy-tale man in the moon. How ridiculous, I thought. How can I speak to this silent Jesus trapped inside a cage?

I knelt alone in front of the mysterious monstrance of seeming contradiction. Here was my loving God who allowed our hearts to get ripped out. Christ was right here in front of me, encircled by flickering candlelight and twin statues of earnestly adoring angels, but he appeared as cold and soundless as Antarctica. Here was my tender Savior who allowed the unrelenting ache into my soul.

Catholic tradition has it that Holy Hour originated as a time for worshippers to make up for the hour in Gethsemane when the apostles chose to go to bed with rocks as their pillows. "Could you not keep watch for one hour?" (Mark 14:37). But for the first few months of Adoration, I was a clock-watcher living in the backwoods of worship. I flung complaints and questions toward the Host in the elevated golden monstrance. And all I ever got in return was the full-moon face of silence. Sixty minutes felt like a sentence.

Then, after a long time, I realized my approach had become both a fruitless exercise in self-indulgence and intolerably boring. So I started opening my eyes. And I saw beautiful things.

I saw Deacon Nick fall fully prostrate on the ground, nose and kneecaps to the floor, with his arms raised above his head and his palms cupped open to catch God's graces. I saw a young man in Birkenstocks pull out a guitar and sing love songs to Christ. I saw a teenage girl sit cross-legged in front of the monstrance and spill tears onto the floor. I noticed that the blond woman who always followed me in my hour of adoration continually arrived twelve minutes early, to kneel in a sustained, rapturous staring contest with the elevated Host.

And by a slow-motion epiphany (grace often arrives that way), the torrent of colorfast images from the failed adoption seemed to recede when I cracked the heavy side door of the church to walk into the Blessed Sacrament's presence. I realized I was again falling in love with this silent Jesus and that I had been going about this all wrong. And once I learned how to properly unload the pain with a genuine belief that he would take it and suitably tend to my brokenness, my voyage to the heart of darkness changed course. I began a gentle joyride back up the river, sort of like the restful journey taken by Huck and Jim.

Kneeling face-to-face with the infinite disproportion of it all—his Body, Blood, Soul, and Divinity wedged into a golden monstrance—I truly did hand all the unholy mess over to him, though not entirely confident that he would usher the pain away. But because Christ is rooted to the deepest breaks in my soul and psyche, he did take it away. All of it. Krista's too.

The centerpiece of his program is love, where his warmhearted tenderness and mercy eclipse the misery of debilitating dead ends. Grace outmuscles guilt and soothes even what seems to be unremitting, bedrock anger. "Come to me, all you who labor and are burdened, and I will give you rest" (Matthew 11:28). I belong to him.

And so did my distress, so I let it all go. And a metamorphosis began to unfold before this Jesus-in-a-Host, Jesus-with-us mystery that surpasses the limits of imagination and human reason. Jesus wasn't lying when he said in John 6:55, "For my flesh is true food, and my blood is true drink."

So what of it? Can it be a sham?

No. Because any person who can wake Lazarus, walk on whitecaps, still the storm, make a fish-and-bread snack into a feast for several thousand, and manage a million other things that a world of books couldn't contain can make bread his own flesh.

The Holy Spirit has no limitations. It just takes faith, that's all.

THE RIVER (TO) SHANNON

Even though adopting our third child continued on its interminably unlucky trek—two more commitments from birth mothers broke off and frittered away—Krista and I were able to hold on to a mysterious peace. God was in control, we knew, so we placed our trust within his providence, continually reminded of what Paul told the Romans: "Affliction produces endurance, and endurance, proven character, and proven character, hope, and hope does not disappoint" (Romans 5:3–5).

Once we were chosen by a couple whose daughter was diagnosed in utero with a clubfoot. I called an old friend, a podiatrist on Maryland's eastern shore. He told me medical advances would have the child's foot in fine condition before she was old enough to start school. He sent us a stack of information on various corrective procedures, which became nightly reading material. Days from the baby's delivery, I was fairly confident I could be the one to perform the surgery.

We flew down to Florida and rented a place by the hospital. Two days before our birth mother was to be induced, we agreed to meet the couple at a local pizza place. We ordered the pizza just after noon. It sat like a manhole until two. The couple never showed.

We learned later that, in fact, their child's foot was actually healthy. False alarm. So after four months of communication and a commitment to place their child with us, the couple left our lives without a whisper—deciding they'd like to keep a more perfect version of their child.

Our four-year run of shipwrecked adoption attempts finally ran its course. A young lady who grew up unloved in a poor part of Florida pointed to a picture of us in a scrapbook. That's them. They're the ones.

Our agency called us one day. You've been chosen, they said. She'd like to meet you this weekend if you're able.

There are some who leave the warmth of the womb for a cold that rarely breaks. Our birth mother was one.

"I saw your pictures, and your children look happy," she said that weekend. "That's what I want for my girl." And we just smiled big smiles, totally unaware of the galaxies of meaning and consequence behind her words.

Later we sat across from her at a restaurant, stunned as she told us the story of her catastrophic childhood. She wanted the opposite for her child, even though she wasn't sure how she would handle the pain in the aftermath of the adoption. And I remembered the words of John the Baptist: "He must increase; I must decrease" (John 3:30).

She told us that "everyone" thought she should keep her baby. For the first six months of her pregnancy, she had agreed with them. The baby's father, a violent man, was out of the picture. Then she started to think. She considered adoption.

When word leaked to her father, he tore into her, saying she was making a "selfish" decision in giving her baby up. Perhaps that told her she was finally doing something right. Her decision firmed. She would place her child for adoption.

I've seen beauty in this world, but it's always rendered microscopic when I pay witness to one act of true sacrifice, the kind that wounds. Humility and meekness are the seats of sacrifice—the first must be last. Perhaps that's why this quiet young lady, so in need of love, decided to do what she did. When she handed Shannon to Krista, she sobbed deeply for a long time. Some things you never get over. I'll never forget her mourning.

But now, several years later, I know this woman still finds joy in her decision to place her child with us. I hope her sacrifice also gives her a sense of pride and tranquility. One choice can reshape everything. I hope when she looks back on her choice, she realizes that she was, in fact, a hero for her child.

By the way, guess where Shannon—named after Ireland's famous river—was born? Inside that horror house—the same hospital where we failed to find John Paul. The maternity ward was up and running this time. The parking stripes were bright white.

We took SR 62 back. Things were patched up.

U n w e l c o m e   R e t u r n

Back to my brain. It gets bad again.

On a blue-sky summer morning six months after my release from ICU, I walked without worry into the hospital for my first follow-up angiogram. One of the University of Maryland Medical Center's chief neurosurgeons had told me prior to leaving the hospital that there lingered only a 2 percent chance that an arteriovenous malformation would return to the wounded real estate in my cerebellum. His prognosis had allowed a ray of sunshine into my life.

"Live your life as normally as you wish, and be patient," he had told me back in the cold hours of the January morning, when my partially shaved, pounding head was still thick with surgery's aftershock. "In a year or so, the balance and headache issues you're experiencing today will be gone. You will be just like your old self." His words were like a song.

As the surgeon stood at the foot of my bed, I was just learning how to cope with the headaches. The Byzantine guest that scheduled appointments every two or so hours possessed alarming power. Though there were other discomforts while I was bedridden in ICU, the head pain eclipsed the others and continually sidetracked my recovery.

DISCOVERY

After I was administered general anesthesia that July morning, a narrow catheter was gently threaded through an artery in my groin toward its destination at the rear of my brain. This would be the fourth—and thankfully the last, I was thinking at the time—navigation of my brain's hazardous frontiers.

But after the procedure was completed, I received a hay-maker: The AVM had returned.

An array of thin blood vessels was beginning to feather around the problem artery in the exact location of my hemorrhage. Like stampeding sin, the renegade artery was recruiting and attaching itself to others. It was assuming an insidious personality, like a Lazarus-turned-bully no one wanted back.

It's funny. When weighty issues like these rise up, men's thoughts often rocket to their wives. I suppose we never really shake our primordial, hair-trigger desire to diffuse a grave matter and spin away its weightiness. I imagine this reaction dates back to our forefathers five thousand generations removed, who cheerfully explained to their lady that the disfiguring torso wound from the pterodactyl mauling was merely a nick.

But my wife is not stupid. I sorta am.

Shortly after the bad news was sprung, I told Krista what had been told to me: that a successful treatment called

"Gamma Knife" could blast the bad blood vessels away and finally put a stake in the protracted drama.

"Gamma what?" she asked, visibly distraught over the return of the AVM.

"Gamma Knife. A neurosurgeon's gonna place a metallic crown on my head, insert some screws, then launch 201 beams of radiation into my brain, to blast the AVM away. It sounds bad, Krista, but it's not," I said. "Other than the crown, I won't feel a thing.

"And get this," I added, like a cheerful caveman. "I get released either later that day or, at worst, the next."

But my rendering of the Gamma Knife wasn't a fait accompli. It doesn't have a foolproof success rate—nowhere near it. And I wouldn't know if the radiation treatment did the trick until roughly eighteen months after the procedure had been administered. Essentially I would be living with the AVM for a while longer. And I knew it could spring a leak at any moment. The doctor told me so.

On the ride home after receiving the startling news, we stopped to pick up Sean at a summer baseball camp. We were able to watch the last hour of practice, sprawled out on a cool, grassy berm that ran parallel to the right-field line. Talk between us was minimal as we watched Sean, one of the universe's tallest six-year-olds, field grounders from third base, where he unsuccessfully attempted to blend in with kids much older than he. As ball met aluminum and baseball chatter spilled to all corners of the manicured field, our minds were on the miasma inside my brain.

My third baseman thought I would be at work on this random weekday in the early afternoon. So when he saw me watching from far off on the sloping hill, he smiled deeply.

A kid at shortstop, four or so years older than my son, screamed something critical at Sean when he missed a ball hit sharply to his left. Sean was left wordless, arms at his sides, uncertain how to respond to getting chewed out by an older boy he didn't know. And my eyes began to water, because I knew life was moving along and there were some things I couldn't do anything about.

After practice we stopped at a tiny clapboard snow-cone stand across the street from the high school field and ordered up the biggest ones they served. Sean got blue raspberry. We talked baseball and sucked on our snow cones until we got home.

"Dad, why'd you come today?" Sean asked, bright blue stains marking his face and tongue.

"Easy one," I said. "Because I love you."

The Face of Christ

A few weeks later Krista and I were summoned back to the hospital for a full day of consultations with radiologists, neurosurgeons, and the hospital's Gamma Knife specialist, a pleasant-tempered neurosurgeon who had already set a date at summer's end to perform the procedure. We had a ninety-minute break after meeting with a radiologist who unfolded the mysteries behind the 201 beams of consolidated radiation that would attempt to scab up the malformation and incrementally eviscerate it.

With some time to spare, we made the easy decision to leave the hospital and walk four blocks north to order up Dagwood-thick crab cake sandwiches at Lexington Market, the famous 125-year-old Baltimore landmark dropped into a now-tough area of the city. On the walk over, I was once again reminded of the abundance of blessings in my life. I saw a man with one ear lying on the ground near the gravesite of Edgar Allan Poe. Two cussing women were engaged in a vicious argument over money. We walked past several street people with dirty Styrofoam coffee cups and small signs requesting donations. I smiled warmly at the first handful of beggars and said, "God bless you," but eventually I tried to pick up the pace as more and more of them came into view.

If an enormous comic strip bubble had managed to bob above those four blocks of asphalt, it may have read, "Lord, why this pain?" But it's on every corner, in every alleyway, and right in front of us within our own homes. Whether we're in the throes of suffering in a hospital room or sprawled out on a city street corner, it's difficult getting past the fact that it often seems as if God just isn't there. But he is. In fact, I've now come to believe, his presence is more abundant in our suffering than at any other time—because very often this is when the magical power of prayer can swoop in and tenderly lift us.

But how does prayer reach the friendless, earless street man? This man has no angelus bell to drop him to a knee in thanksgiving and praise. His worn-out guardian angel repeatedly whispers, "Wake up, wake up, my love, and let him in," but this man has been demolished by life and doesn't hear the beckoning. His angels are demons, continually taunting him with reasoned reminders of his worthlessness and rotten-egg existence, which they tell him can never be unscrambled.

Why does this lonely man suffer? What can I possibly do for this man?

I can pray for him and love him. Because in a mysterious, confounding way, God answers each of our prayers. He promised.

I was lucky when I was thought to be dying. Fifty Masses were said for me in Ireland, and countless others throughout the States. Someone lit a candle for me at the Vatican; at the same time a college friend told me a Mass was being offered for me in the Middle East. I can't tell you the number of people who've told me they said rosaries to lend ancillary aid in my distress. I was given a stockpile of healing oils and a tidal wave of sanctified waters from Padre Pio, Bethlehem, Lourdes, and Fatima.

But what of the earless recluse lying in a puddle of broken glass? He has no bottle of Lourdes water; he'd probably sell it. He assuredly is the leper two thousand years later. He is the prostitute, the blind man, the broken man who came into the Samaritan's view—the same collection of outcasts whom Jesus looked on with so much pity.

I believe the earless man is the very man Christ has enabled me, specifically, to encounter, to stoop down to, to look affectionately in the eye, and to love. It's at that moment, I believe, that I am the answer to someone's old, whispered prayer for this beaten man. I am the face of Jesus Christ for him. I believe we all are, if we allow this confounding prayer to reach its finishing point.

After lunch Krista and I headed back to the hospital for more consultations. On the way we walked past one of Baltimore's many antique Catholic churches: St. Jude—the patron saint of hopeless cases.

THE SHAPE OF DIVINE LOVE

After a second doctor's consultation, we attended Mass at the small, multidenominational "worship space" on the ground floor of the hospital. I used to watch this same Mass unfold from the small television set in my ICU room. I looked forward to the split second before Mass when pretty Krista would walk past the camera to find a seat in the tiny worship room. Six months later it felt heartening to be on the other end of the television screen.

For some time I had wanted to go back to the ICU floor to thank the cadre of nurses who had helped resurrect me. I wanted to see two specifically, John and Stephanie. So for the first time since I was freed from my four-week stay in ICU, I hit the 7 button on the elevator.

Immediately I heard the laugh down the hall. It was the spontaneous, pleasantly pitched, salvific laugh of John, the laugh that somehow managed daily to penetrate the ICU floor's thick wall of despair. When Krista and family and friends weren't permitted in, John was my oasis. He was the lighthearted teddy bear with wire-rimmed glasses and short bushy hair and the unwitting owner of Baltimore's most genuine smile.

Near the end of my stay in ICU, it was John who pushed me to get out of bed and finally take my first few steps with the aid of his powerful arms and a walker. "Come on, you wimp," he said, with that goofy laugh that carried across the floor like a breeze reaching Golgotha's heights. "Get your butt out of bed. Let's go. We have a tour to take."

When we shuffled past the nurses' station, I received a round of applause from the smiling nurses, and I teared up. It was the first time I had taken a step since I put my kids to bed that fateful January night.

"Oh, come on, ladies," he said. "You're making Kevin blush."

Six months later I was calling out his name. John stopped and studied my face for a second or two. "Those eyes," he said. "Can't forget those eyes." Then he embraced me with his teddy bear hug. And my eyes began to get watery again, a few footsteps from where he had led me on that healing tour. Over his shoulder I saw the room, my room. The curtains were drawn, and it was dark.

I thanked John for helping to heal me. I told him of the large role he had played in advancing my recovery, for which I would never be able to properly express my gratitude. I told him he was brilliant with the Gillette when he shaved my face.

What I didn't tell him was that he had daily managed to pull me from my black valley of suffering by simply drawing the curtains and walking into my room. Although it seemed all the nurses did their best to care for me, John was different. The outpouring of his intimacy and care seemed to spring straight from his soul—which is precisely what I needed when my spirit was buried in a coffin. He radiated the divine. And because he did, my desolate landscape always had a pinhole of light.

I was lucky: Stephanie also was working that day. John called her over. "Hey, remember this guy?" he hollered. "The one with the brain issue back in the winter? Kevin."

Stephanie gave me a once-over, then saw Krista standing beside me. It clicked. She walked up and gave my wife a long, warm embrace; then I got the same loving gift. Krista has a special love for Stephanie. She believes that I'm alive because of her.

One afternoon Stephanie had discovered that my shunt was clogged. The fluids that were supposed to be draining were instead drowning my brain. She instantaneously summoned Gary, the mild-manned, kind-faced neurosurgeon who was on call. Within minutes the pair were working feverishly to burrow another shunt into a different location on my head.

What I remember are the wild hallucinations I was having as they were grinding the shunt into place. I thought I was driving my truck down the beltway in Virginia with a thick, gauzy net covering my face. (Stephanie had placed a cloth over my head to prevent infection during the frantic procedure.) I believed that Stephanie was my cousin Cara, who had visited me earlier in the day, and I kept pleading with her to get the net off my face because it was suffocating me. Plus, I begged, I couldn't see the oncoming traffic. I thought Gary and Stephanie were in the back seat of my truck, reaching over the console to drive something into my skull.

(Ah, those hallucinations. I once told Dad to let the Baltimore Orioles baseball team into my room. I told him they had been waiting patiently in the hallway and that it was OK for them to enter. I told him another time that one of my uncles, who was probably at home enjoying dinner at the time, had just died. One day I directed my brother Colin to handle some work issues at a series of jobs that didn't exist. I asked another brother, Mike, to get my briefcase from the other room. I have never in my life owned a briefcase.)

Stephanie was another who radiated the divine love of Christ. She could crack a corny joke and help guide a shunt into my skull in unison. She'd drop old-world Polish vernacular into breezy conversations while tenderly stripping away my oily garments to bathe me. When the pain seemed insurmountable, she found a way to rub life back into my shoulders, arms, and legs. She owned that secret signature of love by which everything she offered me, it seemed, came straight from the gentlest part of her soul.

Stephanie and John, I believe, were God's direct answer to prayers for me—two daisies fighting up through a scorched landscape. Theirs were the earthly skin, touch, and power that completed the prayer channel, conveying God's miraculous healing to my poor, wounded body.

chapter ten

Vacation Realizations

I had planned a vacation at a charming place buried in the Green Mountains of Vermont a few weeks prior to the Gamma Knife procedure. The day before backing our minivan out of the driveway, a phone call came in from a neurosurgeon at the Cleveland Clinic, a center of excellence for issues of the brain. The wife of one of my cousins had a close working relationship with the clinic and had kindly helped arrange a review of my stack of angiograms and MRIs.

I was at the office late in the afternoon making out an invoice and discussing job sites with my brothers Dan and Colin when the surgeon introduced himself over the phone. After exchanging pleasantries, he emphasized that our conversation would be a subtlety-free zone and encouraged me to ask anything.

"Well," I managed for starters, "is it as bad as I've been told?"

"I'm looking at it now," he said in a helpful but direct tone, "and it looks like there's a one-in-five chance of it rupturing within the next year."

"Oh," I managed. "It hasn't been told to me like that before. Uh, if it bursts, do you think I'll have the awareness to contact emergency?"

"Maybe," he said. "But it could bring death."

New England's mountainscape would be taking on a different luster.

After hanging up I decided to keep the news temporarily wrapped from Krista, though it instantly felt beyond my holding capacity. On the drive home that night, I prayed the rosary with watery eyes. Rather than relying on my customary personal frontiers of the five sorrowful mysteries, I summoned the contemplative landscape from my hospital days—the calming one that had my head in Christ's lap within a circle of children.

I pulled into my driveway and saw my own children immersed in the ritualistic glories of a young person's summer. Gabby and her friend Julia were splashing their kaleidoscope of Raphael and Monet chalk masterpieces on the sidewalk. Sean was awaiting my arrival in the side yard, throwing himself pop-ups, which he circled beneath like a miniature Willie Mays patrolling center field at the Polo Grounds. My old Rawlings glove and a baseball awaited me in the driveway, in the exact spot where Sean knew my truck would roll in.

My friendly neighbor Carlos waved me in after retrieving his mail and stopped to say hello. "Natives are restless for Daddy," he said.

"Best part of the day," I said, eyes bloodshot.

Sean raced over and shoved my mitt into my gut at the same time that Gabby requested I give her sidewalk tour de force a once-over. I knew Krista was inside preparing dinner, which would be served in fifteen minutes. Once again I was overwhelmed by the royalty of family life. Two steps out of my truck, and the diary of disturbance written in the lines of my face was rewritten by a joy sprung from my soul's warmest place.

Like tidal breezes, autumn pennant chases, and Guinness served in low-ceilinged pubs, the tangible richness of family is more motivation for me to believe that God's fingerprints are all over this place—and that he loves us so. By its very essence on this day, family allowed the shackles of my weariness to melt away and be replaced by an opportunity to love.

"Sean," I said, kicking my boots off, "this one's going really high. Make sure your glove's on tight. It's hittin' Jesus' beard."

New World

My thirty-four-year-old cousin Tommy is generous. Earlier in the summer he and his wife, Molly, had offered his kingdom of cousins weekend access to their elegant condominium overlooking a shimmering expanse of the Hudson River and the Statue of Liberty. So we spent the weekend in New York City before heading to Vermont.

Tom's place is a short stroll from the splash of bohemian restaurants, pubs, and shops of Greenwich Village. But Gabby found the brownstone down the street—the same one where the Huxtables "lived" in *The Cosby Show*—more thrilling on our walk to the pizza parlor.

Krista wasn't fond of my strolls with the children.

One weekday night two weeks earlier, I had been out with my youngest, Shannon, in our cul-de-sac. A friendly neighbor invited me in for some lemonade and offered to hold Shannon in her lap for a while. I joked with her two kids and listened to the latest news on her husband, who was in the midst of a sixteen-month overseas assignment with the military. As the last shades of sunlight retreated beneath the shingled rooftops and towering oaks of Crofton, I thanked my friend for the company and walked across the street to put Shannon to sleep and watch a few innings of the Orioles game with Sean.

I walked in to see Krista, Gabby, and Sean sitting in a rigid line on the couch in our living room—a room we did not frequent but one that offered a perfect view of the gentle rhythm of our neighborhood. Gabby—whom I call my Little Flower because of her Samaritan soul—jumped off the couch, ran at me, and asked in an unfamiliar, pleading tone, "Dad, where were you?"

Puzzled, I looked to Krista and saw tears in her eyes. Oh, man.

"What in the world's going on in here?" I managed.

I saw Gabby look into Krista's eyes, awaiting her reply. Our poor little sweetheart, bewildered by her mommy's distress, had no idea what it would be, because Krista and I have done our best to immunize her and Sean from the black issues inside my head.

Krista regained her composure and, in a measured tone, sought to soften the room's heightened atmosphere. "Kevin, we were just worried about you," she said with increasing nonchalance. "You just sort of disappeared on us."

When Krista's maternal instinct told her the room had been properly pulled back together, she shuffled the kids into the family room. She told me to hold still. Oh, man.

With Gabby and Sean out of earshot, Krista cracked open a gateway of revelation for me. "You have got to tell me where you are going when you have Shannon with you," she said, again on the verge of tears. "I didn't know anything. You could have been on the ground, and Shannon could have been in the middle of the road."

I knew then that the curtains had closed on a part of my life. Bluster about "just being across the street" would ring hollow. I had blown it. Krista understood that the repercussions of another thunderclap headache and AVM burst could lead to my infant daughter being lost and alone, possibly in the middle of the road. I vowed to Krista that I wouldn't screw up again while cradling Shannon.

As I lay in bed that night, I tried to square my guilt and manufacture reasons to secure my everyday independence. But I realized that until the day a surgeon told me, "It's gone forever," I couldn't escape the tighter bounds of my new reality. I resided in new country now, where my thoughts and actions could no longer run breezily along.

I knew I would awaken in the morning in that newly birthed wilderness of always placing myself second—not necessarily the worst thing in the world. Before drifting off to sleep, I thanked God for my wife, who was dreaming beside me, because I knew she loved me and saw the simple things I couldn't.

GRACE ON THE HUDSON

After enjoying a night of textbook New York pizza, drinking a glass of good Chianti, and staring into the city nightscape with my awestruck kids, I awakened at daybreak and walked across West Street to a bench on the shores of the Hudson River. Morning sunlight cut through a turquoise blue sky, and a soft breeze promised a fine Saturday. Ferries were chugging their daily routes out to Staten Island. Yellow water taxis passed by early risers in the first sailboats to rock the small waves.

Determined joggers raced past, giving me head nods and whispering, "Good morning." I could hear the faint blare from their iPods as they rushed past and out of view.

After reading the Magnificat's morning prayer, the day's reading, the Gospel, and the daily meditation, I opened *The Wall Street Journal* and came across perhaps the most heartening article I've ever read. The piece, "A Different Kind of Miracle on the Hudson," written by Fr. Jonathan Morris, detailed the catastrophe that had occurred one week earlier within view of where I was sitting.

A helicopter and small plane had collided over the Hudson, and the aftermath was nine dead. Captain Jeremy Clarke had been carrying five Italian tourists in his helicopter on a delightful Saturday afternoon when he was struck by the plane. As the blare of fire engines and police cars filled the streets alongside the Hudson, a miracle of no small magnitude unfolded.

Fr. Morris, who was an eyewitness to the crash, inherited the delicate role of counselor for the grieving families in the days following the tragedy. What he went on to behold was remarkable. Instead of listening to the harrowing echo of untold suffering, he played witness to a radical kind of grace that sprung from the souls and out of the mouths of mourning family members. For the week following the tragedy, Fr. Morris remained awed by the demonstration of forgiveness and humility.

Captain Clarke, who had recently gotten engaged to a beautiful young lady, had just returned to his Catholic faith and received the sacrament of confirmation. He had recently written a "letter to God," which his fiancée shared with Fr. Morris.

> Dear God,
> None of this [his newfound love and engagement] could have happened without your intervention. The timing could not have been more perfect. The improbable has become a reality.
>
> I pray to keep improving myself and getting better with your help. Thank you for all that I have in my life, I am blessed.
>
> With love,
> Jeremy Clarke

Fr. Morris went on to write, "Capt. Clarke's mother, Beatrice, a woman of profound spirituality, had been praying for his return to the faith for many years. 'It was the perfect time,' she told me, not knowing her words echoed her son's."

The article included a message from Clarke's and his fiancée's extended families: "Please, please get the message to the families of the Italian tourists who were on

Jeremy's helicopter how much we grieve for them. How sorry we are. And please, please tell the family of the pilot and passengers of the small plane, that no matter the outcome of the investigation, we hold no hard feelings. We are suffering with them too."

Amazingly, the relatives of the deceased Italian tourists responded with similar outpourings of grace and forgiveness.[1]

All of us, it seems to me as I grow older, are confronted with at least one tragic event. And working through the aftermath of those tragedies is where we will determine every future instance of our lives.

After reading this article, the meaning of the cross came to mind. As the Blessed Mother, Mary Magdalene, and John stood like a trinity of devastation before their tortured Savior, two things could have occurred: the dawn of a deep poverty of soul and psyche, or the decision to yield to the Holy Spirit in their broken-heartedness. Three days later Mary Magdalene was the first to see the Risen Christ; seven weeks later the Blessed Mother and John were Pentecost ringleaders.

The decision of the Blessed Mother, Mary Magdalene, and John to plod forward after the gruesomeness of the cross was repeated in the radical decision to forgive and move on made by the families of Jeremy Clarke and the visiting Italians. In a sense they, too, stood sentinel before the horror of the cross. And because they seemed to understand that Christ allowed—not injected—the tragedy into their lives, thousands of *Wall Street Journal* readers on that sunny morning received a glimpse into the depth of grace and the astonishing manner in which it can prevail over the unquiet sea of pain.

Alpine Idiocy

Of course I had been praying with greater frequency. It's really something walking around aware that thuggish blood vessels in your head could cause instant death with your next step. Prayer, like a greasy pizza pie at 2 AM for a fraternity kid, can be a natural and delicious recourse.

But here's the thing I'm learning about prayer: No matter how often I reach out for Christ or call on my favorite saint, I can easily perform a mind-bendingly idiotic act to render all of it obsolete.

In Killington, Vermont, Sean and I discovered Herbert I. Johnson Field, America's most beautiful Little League baseball diamond. A mountain stream flows along the right-field line, and a tree-lined mountain rises up like a proud father just beyond the outfield. During those August days an explosion of wild flowers lay beyond the right-center-field fence. The grass was greener than Kinsella's Iowa ballpark, and there were no weeds. The field looked as if it was being maintained by Norman Rockwell and Doubleday descendants.

Sean and I visited the diamond every day of our vacation. We ran the bases (well, Sean ran the bases), practiced "diamond divers" (meaning Sean had to lunge for grounders before throwing to first base), and hit baseballs into wide-open spaces. We had the place to ourselves.

One morning we saw a groundskeeper, and I complimented him on his field.

"Yeah," he said, "we take some pride in this one."

After assuring us it was OK to use his field, he asked Sean if he had visited the alpine slide up the road. The man had my son's attention when he described it as one of the longest slides in the country. I think excitement caused Sean to lose his breath a little as the man spoke of the hairpin turns, dips, tricky *S*-turns, and alarming speed of the straightaways. Within a minute the baseball gear was loaded up, and we were racing off to "Pico." It was there that I would reveal again how lopsided and short-sighted my thoughts can be.

We saw after stepping off the chair lift that the alpine slide offered two tracks. Since we are boys, this of course generated the question, "Wanna race?"

"Oh, yeah, Dad," my son said.

If a candle had been in my back pocket, I would have started waxing the bottoms of our sleds. As it was, the smack talk hit high gear rather quickly.

"Seriously, Sean," I intoned with the solemnity of Solomon, "if you're having second thoughts, we could always take the chairlift back down."

"Yeah, Dad," Sean said, knowing his father too well. "Sure."

"If you're starting to get nervous, I think I can find one of Shannon's pacifiers in the car seat," I offered.

"Sure, Dad," Sean responded, grinning. "If you need one, go ahead."

As we slid onto our sleds, I told Sean I would be waiting for him at the bottom with lunch. He laughed at that one.

Three. Two. One.

"Hey, Sean. Let's roll!"

Midway down my six-year-old was walloping me.

In an effort to save face, I jammed my throttle forward—a rather unwise act for a man heading into a banked hairpin turn with a recently glued brain. I lost control, and my sled jettisoned off the track. My head thwacked against the side of the slide; it felt as if it had been cudgeled.

After a few minutes of realization that I was likely to live, I hopped back on the sled and slowly navigated my way down the mountain. En route I considered what might have been the lead story in the next day's edition of *The Mountain Times:*

> *Brain Patient Loses His Mind*
> Kevin Wells, 41, who recently underwent emergency brain surgery in Baltimore, died after sustaining a massive head injury while taking a banked turn too rapidly at the Pico Mountain Alpine Slide. His son, Sean Thomas Wells, 6, who accompanied him to the slide on Tuesday, was left without a father because of Mr. Wells's daring run. "Dad really wanted to beat me," said the fatherless boy.

Upon my arrival at the bottom of the mountain, Sean should have been shimmying like Michael Jackson in an end zone. But he saw the considerable pink welt beneath my left eye.

"Dad, what happened?" he asked, an oversized Orioles cap shading his bright blue eyes.

"Um," I explained.

"Uh," he said, "ready for the next ride?"

"Wouldn't miss it for the world," I said.

As we hopped back on the chairlift for our charming taxi ride back to the mountain peak, I inventoried the damage. Badly shredded knees and elbows and a ringing head with a scrape the size of Goliath's thumbprint.

"Sean, your Dad's going to take it easier this time."

"Aw, Dad.... Let's go get that pink pacifier."

My misadventure reminded me once again of my tendency to listen to my own voice instead of God's. Three days after promising Krista I would give my actions more forethought, I took a chainsaw to the vow. Truly, it was a gutter-ball decision. Another one. But here's my saving grace: Grace.

With grace I can salvage the gutter balls by knocking down a few pins on my next approach. With meaningful and prayerful pleas for his grace, I know I can eventually proceed to roll a spare, then ring up a fine collection of strikes, and eventually have myself a near perfect game. But void of his saving graces and the steadfast yearning for its sacredness within me, I will bowl my life away with the proficiency of the president of our country.

I know myself and my sinfulness too well, and the quest for sainthood often seems like tilting at windmills. But if I decide to continue to root myself in prayer and make the Spirit-fueled graces of the sacraments truly abundant in my life, I know my aim will at least have a pulse. And life will unfold with greater luster.

I know this because the fruits of the Holy Spirit—the spiritual Swiss army knife of love, joy, peace, patience, kindness, generosity, faithfulness, gentleness, and self-control—are at least taking seed and helping to orchestrate a more lyrical rhythm to my life. I regard this Advocate whom Christ promised as sort of a pom-pom–waving cheerleader spurring me on from the sidelines of my soul. "I will ask the Father, and he will give you another Advocate to be with you always," Jesus told his saucer-eyed apostles (John 14:16).

"Grace perfects nature," St. Thomas Aquinas taught. To me it's the greatest three-word sentence ever uttered, because it means there's hope for all of us, even the chronic gutter-ballers.

And it's the reason there's even a chance for me, after notifying Sean, on our second taxi up the mountain, of the three blood-stained zombies still alive within the embalming room in the black basement of Glenn Dale Hospital, the old tuberculosis ward where my friends and I used to trespass as teenagers.

Boy, his mercy better be wide.

chapter eleven

Night of Lights

I was still walking job sites like a Wisconsin logroller because of my sliced cerebellum when my brother Dave and I stepped into a roadside chicken restaurant on a searing summer afternoon. The aroma of sweat and rotisserie chicken ricocheted with the steam off the walls and enveloped us, while the stares of several diners and red-faced cooks, the cashier, and a busboy zeroed in on Dave, the slender young seminarian in black standing beside me. The enormity of his radical decision to hand over his life fully and completely to God was reawakened within me like a rare August breeze.

Dave looked like a wide-eyed little boy as he ordered his two-piece dark chicken platter and Coke. Although I knew his lifelong vocation was only in its infancy, I had been convinced for some time that he had comfortably found his dwelling place.

It had been five years since Dave sat across from me in an old booth at legendary Ledo's Pizza in Adelphi, Maryland. There he told me and a family priest friend, Fr. Mario, that he had made the decision to enter the seminary following his graduation from the University of Maryland. We ordered a carafe of red wine, and the night took flight.

"I don't know. I just kind of always saw how happy Tommy was as a priest and how many lives he touched," Dave said that night. "And I think the priesthood is something I'd really enjoy."

Ledo's was one of my Uncle Tommy's favorites. It's wedged into the heart of an ancient strip mall and down the road from one of his old parishes and the University of Maryland. Pitchers of beer are cheap, pizza is oily, and diners are hardscrabble. In other words, Ledo's offered the perfect, no-frills sanctum for Tommy to help equip a college kid with the navigational tools necessary to confront the innumerable intersections of morality and college life.

The magical evening that Dave shared the news with us, Tommy had been dead for four years. But his lanky frame seemed to be seated alongside us in our worn, cozy booth—laughing at our toasts, rejoicing in his nephew's commitment, and sharing fully in our delight. Since his death, I don't know if I had ever felt his presence more than on that night.

Tough Assignment

The afternoon we had lunch, Dave was in his fourth year at Mount St. Mary's, one of America's largest seminaries, tucked like a painting into the rolling green mountains of western Maryland. But I still regarded him as the smiling kid brother who posed palming a pint of Guinness with a stout mustache in a seaside Ireland pub. He was the little boy who sweated out my nightly "Closet Monster" bed-time stories along with brothers Mike, Colin, and John. He cringed in the passenger seat of the "Milachi Speedburner"—my first car, a coal-black '78 Datsun 280Z that hugged my old neighborhood roads at unsafe speeds. He was still a toddler in a high chair when I headed out for a high school date.

Dave was the one Tommy tagged as "the one." I'm not sure how he knew.

Dave is a terrific basketball and soccer player. He has an understated, easy wit and is fluent in Spanish and beloved by children. He'll be required to bring those gifts and many more into a vocation that will beg him to become a man—a true man, like St. Peter upside-down on the cross or John Wayne pushing past a saloon's swinging doors. He'll need to be entirely unafraid to carry a muscular type of evangelization into his ministry.

He'll be asked to impart the towering truth of the magis-terium into the stiff head winds of a culture that will often prove ambivalent, uneager, or even too angry to receive it. Heavy-breathing secularists, agnostics, rationalists, dissi-dents, and lukewarm and "enlightened" Catholics are just a smattering of groups that will either reject or politely diminish the definitive truths his faith will require him to proclaim.

Thankfully Dave's equipped himself well. He's made Holy Hour the centerpiece of his young life. For five years he has decided to go straight to Jesus Christ in the Blessed Sacrament to steel and sustain him for the multitude of dis-turbances on the other side of his seminary windowpane.

He knows a large share of his lifelong commitment to Christ will involve confrontations with the unyielding grind of sin. And because he knows there's no charmed, dot-to-dot formula in confronting the growing moral sewer, he's chosen to kneel alone in front of the exposed Blessed Sacrament on a daily basis to ask for discernment on how to face it.

Daily Adoration is an unusual devotion for anyone in this world. Dave, like all of us, needs Christ. And wonderfully, when he's face-to-face with the Real Presence in meditation, prayer, and openness, Christ is enabling him to incrementally develop in wisdom, humility, love, and character. Dave goes to Christ because Christ is his Shepherd. He goes because of Christ's promise of sanctifying graces. He goes to worship, grow, and give thanks.

This young man of twenty-six, who looked all of sixteen on that sweltering summer afternoon, was on the razor's edge of a commitment that will require him to become a hero, emissary, lover, and apostle for Jesus Christ and his Catholic Church. "So we are ambassadors for Christ," St. Paul told his growing church, "as if God were appealing through us" (2 Corinthians 5:20).

It was pretty cool seeing his ambassadorship take shape at the chicken restaurant without his having to whisper a word. Dressed in collar and black, my kid brother told the small story of his fidelity to Jesus Christ simply by filling his soda at the fountain. The curious eyes of diners, picking at their chicken before obligations summoned them back to the demands of their workday, remained fixed on him. One diner in particular didn't seem fond of the ultra-young seminarian sauntering in from the heat. And the words of Tommy—the ones he shared with me two nights before he was murdered—bore into me.

"Kevin," he had said, squaring his shoulders and looking me in the eye, "you are called to be a modern-day martyr now. You might not have to die for your faith in the ways you and I consider true martyrdom, but you are called to become a holy fool in today's world. You can expect to be mocked and ridiculed as you live out your faith. And as that unfolds, Kevin, it will indicate to you that you're taking your faith seriously."

"You know, you should go and see Fr. Stack," Dave said with greasy fingers. "He told me the other day, 'Dave, we might joke around a lot about things, but something very powerful happened in the hospital room that night when I saw Kevin.'"

It had been six months since I'd seen Fr. Jim Stack. In January, when matters turned their gravest, he drove the hour north to Baltimore from his parish in Hyattsville, Maryland, navigated past my cadre of rooters in the lobby of the ICU floor, and walked into the darkness of my room.

The day prior my surgeon had perforated my skull and cerebellum in a failed embolization attempt. After sewing up the back of my head, he had said he wasn't sure what he could do to remove the AVM or trapped blood. He didn't know how to heal me.

Some thought I would die that day. So Stack hopped in his car.

STACKMAN

Like most good priests, Fr. Stack is as rubrical as Redd Foxx and as sacrosanct as a butcher. Stocky, ruddy-cheeked, and of average height, he could easily pass for a retired hockey player.

He doesn't smell of incense, and he'll never whoosh by in ecclesiastical, flowing robes with his nose turned toward Polaris. Some of his black button-downs have holes in the sleeves; they fit though, so who cares?

If you rang Fr. Stack's rectory doorbell at night, embroiled in a crisis, you might find yourself on a walk down the hilly street to Franklin's, where Stack would flick out his collar, order a few Bud longnecks, and try to back-door the Holy Spirit into your mess. He wouldn't sweeten your troubles with rationalizations and loopholes though. Because he knows that what his faith teaches is inde-fectibly holy and good, he'd come at you with callous truths, then offer spiritual mechanisms to help steer you through your dark night.

Fr. Stack is the poster priest for St. Jerome, his flannel-shirted parish buried in a working-class section of Maryland. The old church rests on a hill and is bordered by an old railroad line, a corner pub, squeezed-in antique homes, and bail bondsman outfits. Bruce Springsteen could cut a double album there.

When I plopped down on his rectory couch on a rainy night last fall, he looked like a beaten man. He swept the length of his face with his meaty palm and wondered aloud how he was going to raise the hundred thousand dollars necessary to save his ancient parish school, which was losing students in the teeth of the dark economy. He had just been told by archdiocesan leaders that he had two months to raise the money. If he couldn't get it done, his school could be closed.

"Man. So many good things are going on at that school right now. Got a great principal, good teachers, some really good families involved there," he said. "But that's a bunch of money.... Kevin, I can hear your uncle now: 'It's all about faith, Stack. It's all about faith.'" He was smiling, sort of, at his singsong, mocking imitation of one of Tommy's favorite axioms.

He's free to mock. Tommy was his best friend. As young priests, both drew assignments to Sacred Heart Church in Bowie, Maryland, where they served at separate times under the legendary Msgr. John Hogan—once one of Washington, D.C.'s toughest prep athletes. As a priest Hogan's gruff, doctrinaire manner duplicated his style of trucking over nose guards and linebackers as a star center at powerhouse Gonzaga High School. As an all-metropolitan catcher with a fire-hose arm, he had bruised baseballs and stared down base runners cocky enough to try and steal on him.

Hogan came at congregants hard when heralding his views on all matters Catholic, and at times they were ill-equipped to handle his frankness. His homilies were as elegant as a lumberjack's would be, but his booming message was as sound and unbending as a redwood.

I imagine no priest in America said a faster Our Father. He once tossed me out of confession because I wore shorts. (I was eight and on my way home from the neighborhood pool.) Hogan was a certifiable throwback, an honest relic and sturdy bridge to the priesthood's old-style ways. But he was adored in a unique way because of it.

"Tommy was my spiritual mentor," Fr. Stack said, "and he gave me some great tips on how to handle Hogan."

My uncle and Stackman shared a famous friendship. Because they were funny, personable, streetwise lovers of their vocation, they were able to reach a wide variety of people. Instead of waving a pathetic flag of surrender when challenged by modern-day sin, they fought against it, fur flying, hyperaware that grave, stampeding sin puts us on a downward spiral to hell. Understanding that a genuine spiritual life is in the here and now, they put skin into their vocation, meting out spiritual counsel, love, friendship, and warmth whenever they could. And when they came down hard on someone, they benignly merged their toughness with a twinkle.

Wells and Stack got it. The thousands of parishioners who dwelled within the quaint community of Bowie seemed to love them for making the decision to live within the thick of it all.

Reawakening and Renewal

In the span of a week, Stack lost his two best friends. Tommy was murdered just days after Stack's father died. It was like being disemboweled on Monday and having his soul removed on Thursday. Within no time, it seemed, he found himself within the throes of a slow-motion descent into depression.

He was marooned in the brittle flatlands of spiritual dryness—perhaps the most ruthless landscape for a once-active, jubilant priest. But instead of seeking counseling for his depression, he became like a bewildered Simon of Cyrene, hoisting the demands of his pastoral parish work and depression onto his back and trying to white-knuckle past the malaise. For four long years he rolled out of bed with a dark cloud anchored above him.

Predictably Satan eyed a target ripe for his slaughter and eased himself into Stack's disconsolate mix. Stack says a day rarely went by when the devil didn't lift his hammer and attempt to bring it down squarely on Stack's head—manhandling him with temptation, doubt, and lies. Mostly though, Satan's modus operandi was to convince Stack that he was a bad priest and that his faith was dead. Meantime the poor pastor simply wondered if there was a calling and purpose behind his closet crucible.

"I was in bad shape for a very long time. I couldn't feel his presence," Stack said. "And then Satan came to smash and crush my faith. I just didn't want to believe anymore. I went numb. The whole world was continuing, but I was just standing at the bus stop, trying to find a way.

"Then I went on a retreat, and everything changed."

Stack awakened from a nightmare in a retreat hermitage in New Jersey in 2004. In the dream he had been trying to escape a knife-wielding man. He was startled from his sleep with words that would change his life.

"All of a sudden the room got bright, and I heard a voice—a powerfully strong conviction that distinctly told me, 'I'm going to heal you now.... But now people will also need your healing.' It was the Holy Spirit. I've never felt anything like it in my life.... It was easy to get the part about God healing me. That was wonderful. But the other part took some time."

Stackman is a priest with a number of grace-given gifts, but prior to his life-changing retreat, laying hands on the sick and dying was untilled and unconsidered ground. "Embarrassing stuff," he said. "I thought if I came out with that, people would think I was some kind of kook."

So he kicked off his healing ministry with the eagerness of a kindergartner in line for a flu shot, delicately cherry-picking his way through his divine directive. He healed in secret, lest his congregation and friends regard him as a newfangled hollerin', snake-handlin', Flannery O'Connor-imagined, healin' preacher. Occasionally he prayed over an elderly or sick parishioner in the vestibule after Mass or within the friendly confines of his rectory. He often carried a small bottle of holy oil "just in case," but it was buried deep in his pocket, like an unused rosary. Few parishioners were aware of his new ministry.

In 2007, a few years removed from his depression, a rejuvenated Stack traveled to Guadalupe with a friend, Fr. Dan Leary. On a beautiful, sun-splashed morning, he decided to climb Tepeyac Hill, where in 1531 the Blessed Mother appeared to local peasant Juan Diego. In making his way to the summit, Stack said that an overwhelming voice suddenly brought him to tears of humiliation and dread.

"I was convicted by the Holy Spirit in a deep and powerful way. But it was different this time. All of a sudden there was a loud inner voice that clearly said to me, 'You're grieving me! I'm ashamed of you!' The Holy Spirit let me know that I was afraid of healing and that he was saddened by it. And I felt like a little kid, ashamed and flawed.

"He said, 'I gave you this gift of healing, and you're not using it. I need you to heal now. If not, I'll take it away.'"

After regaining his bearings, Fr. Stack slowly continued his climb. When he reached the summit, something remarkable occurred: The Blessed Mother addressed him with the sweetest, most tender words of reassurance: "Do not be afraid. If you entrust your ministry to me, I will take care of you. Let me take care of the Holy Spirit."

"It was those words that finally empowered me," Stack said.

He returned to his parish emboldened, quickly assembled a team of ushers and catchers, and placed an item in the bulletin: "Healing Mass. Sunday, 4:00 PM." Parishioners did a double take. Stack, a healer? Certainly it was an odd alteration to his personality—like a blacksmith moonlighting as a ballerina. But whereas he once lacked the courage to step out into the unconventional world of healing, Stack now dove in with a passion. Healing others became a prerogative.

Today scores of people know him solely as a minister of healing. Part of that ministry involved his providential visit to me.

LIGHTS

What follows is an account of a divine merging of the mysterious and supernatural, where angels and saints met for one night in a dark room, over a broken head and in a broken situation. What follows is fact, told by a priest who doesn't know how to lie. What follows is another in the long line of miracles that slip through the back door because all the front doors are sealed shut.

When the walls of my life seemed ready to close, Christ threw his arms out and pushed back. He had heard each prayer. Stack, the reluctant, once-clumsy healer, would be his answer.

Here's what Stack said unfolded that night:

He and Mary Pat Donoghue, the principal of his school, who assists in his healing ministry, traveled to Baltimore. En route they prayed the Chaplet of Divine Mercy and initiated their calls on the handful of saints who once walked the cobblestone streets of downtown Baltimore—John Neumann, John Carroll, Elizabeth Ann Seton, and Mother Mary Lange.

Because of my surgical trauma of the previous afternoon, I was incapacitated for most of the day. So Stack and Mary Pat entered my darkened room anticipating a comatose version of myself. Stack approached my bedside and told me he was going to pray over me. He explained how the communion of saints could play a healing role at that time and said he was going to request the intercession of the Baltimore saints. Before igniting his gift though, he asked me which saint I wanted to intercede on my behalf. He was startled by my response.

"Bring my uncle down," I whispered, my first words of the day. "I need Tommy now."

Stack smiled. He then began to call on his best friend, requesting that Tommy come to his nephew's bedside in his moment of need. And Tommy came.

"There were lights everywhere," Stack said. "Everything in your room took on light. And all of a sudden, the presence of Tommy and the saints surrounded you, and everything took on a great warmth. I felt the whole heavenly court around you. It was overwhelming."

Mary Pat, standing alongside Stack, said she felt a powerful, pleasant pulsation, like a warm electrical current, that moved throughout her body. "The whole room got really warm, and I began to get dizzy. I've been assisting Fr. Stack for a while now, but I've never felt what I felt in that room," she said.

My lone memory of the moment is of a sustained, palpable warmth coursing through my chest and abdomen. The heat seemed to settle deep within me. It was like the warmth that gently wrapped around me as a child when I sat on the stone hearth of my grandparents' fireplace after coming in from a Pennsylvania winter night.

So with my uncle and a luminous contingent of the communion of saints apparently crowding my ICU room to intercede on my behalf, something miraculous unfolded. Stack stood in the heart of the lights that were popping all around and continued to anoint my head with oil and pray over me. He had a job to finish. He did it well.

The next day I was given an angiogram. And for the first time, it came back clean. The blood, trapped within my cerebellum for so long, had found a way out. The twisting AVM had vanished.

"The blood has drained," my surgeon said. "You are well."

And I was on my way.

The reach?

Yes.

A VISIT FROM THE BLESSED MOTHER

It's important, I think, to note what occurred in the immediate aftermath of Fr. Stack's departure that night. Two lifelong friends, Dave Tonrey and James Fenton, had
attempted to speak with me two times earlier in the day,
but I had been incapacitated. After Fr. Stack's lengthy visit,
they figured I would be conscious, and so they decided to
give it one last try. Months later James and Dave recounted
on separate occasions what occurred that night, unaware
of its magnitude.

"So we walked in right after Fr. Stack left, and we talked
to you for a while," James said. "And then you were telling
us angels were in the room. Dave and I just kinda looked
at one another, sort of nodding, and we were like, 'Yeah,
uh-huh, we know, Kevin.'"

Then, James told me, I pointed to a corner of the room.
"Look," I whispered. "It's the Lady of Guadalupe."

Makes sense if you think about it.

In Willa Cather's fictional classic *Death Comes for the
Archbishop,* there is a scene in which missionary priest Fr.
Vaillant tries to account for the miracle of Guadalupe to his
bishop friend: "Where there is great love, there is always
miracles," he said. "One might almost say that an apparition is human vision corrected by divine love…so that for
a moment our eyes can see and our ears can hear what is
there about us always."[1]

chapter twelve

Lourdes

The scars on the side of Jim Peck's shaved head seemed to stretch, twist, and meander like rivers on the moon. They told the story of the pair of golf ball–sized tumors pulled from his brain just months before I met him on a pilgrimage to Lourdes in May 2010.

Shortly after fleeing the Icelandic volcanic ash cloud to begin our return flight to BWI Airport in Maryland, I stopped at Jim's seat to visit him. Poor timing. He was in the midst of a seizure.

"Ah, what can you do, Kevin?" he said as his loving wife, Cecilia, tried to comfort him. "It's his way for me."

Sweet Renate (pronounced "Ruh-ná-ta") Klein, whose tiny body began betraying her at seventeen months of age, was a few rows behind Jim. She has one of the world's rarest and most debilitating diseases, ataxia telangiectasia. The recessive genetic disorder has obliterated her coordination and inhibited her motor skills as well as her immune and endocrine systems. AT, it seems, steals a little more each day. Many people with the disorder don't survive beyond puberty, but Renate was twenty-nine and fighting it when she lay prostrate on a thin wooden palette and permitted four foreigners to lower her into the narrow stone bath at Lourdes.

"I had to give myself totally over to people I didn't know," Renate said. "It was very calming and emotionally cleansing to learn that I can surrender myself safely. It was kind of like what I imagine heaven to be like, when all your needs are met."

As her body breached the water, she pulled a statue of the Virgin Mary to her heart, as if it was a life preserver. She heaved and sobbed, her tears mingling with the frigid blessed waters. Then, abruptly, there was silence. Renate knew these were the very waters unearthed by the unlikely tag team of Our Lady and Bernadette—a perfect vessel asking a broken one to root through some dirt in a filthy, forgotten part of the world.

Two rows in front of me on the same flight was an attractive woman named Michelle McKay whose voice is a small miracle. When she sang the Responsorial Psalm at a small Mass at the Church of St. Bernadette a few days before, the congregation was overcome by the melody she managed to pull from her sore upper body. It seemed her soul had dismissed the inelegant arrangement of tumors that stage-four breast cancer had shot all over her torso.

Krista and I were eating pizza one night at a small restaurant when Michelle and her mother slid into the booth beside us. We told Michelle how much her joy shone through her voice.

"I'm happy you saw that," she said. "It came from somewhere inside."

Often when medicine, surgery, and treatment have met their boundaries, people such as Jim, Renate, and Michelle come to the gray stone grotto in Massabielle—an old pigsty that became one of the world's most stunning spots because heaven reached out and touched it. A deprived, undereducated fourteen-year-old named Bernadette Soubirous stepped onto this contaminated piece of land on a winter day in 1858, and it is almost as if a knowing Christ whispered, "Ah, perfect spot, perfect girl."

So the Virgin came down.

MIRACLE IN THE FOOTHILLS

The same year Abraham Lincoln squared off to debate Stephen Douglas, an unemployed miller asked his diminutive, olive-faced daughter to gather firewood at the lonely spot on the outskirts of Lourdes. Bernadette had unfortunately become accustomed to such places. A former jail cell was home to her family of six. On the other side of the iron bars was the neighborhood dunghill. Bernadette went to sleep each night and awoke each morning to the aroma of her neighbors' waste.

While her sister and a friend crossed the Gave River to oblige François Soubirous's request for wood, Bernadette, a weakened asthmatic, hesitated at the river's edge. As she began to remove her stockings and shoes, she heard a rush of wind and noticed some wild rose brambles stirring in a narrow recess above the grotto. Thereafter her world changed.

A resplendent young lady appeared, garbed in white, with a blue sash at her waist. A yellow rose was at each bare foot. The young lady, bathed in a gentle light above a rose bush, smiled at the astonished country girl. This appearance would be the first of eighteen.

Following the eighth apparition, on February 25, 1858, Bernadette reported that she heard the woman say, "Go and drink of the spring and wash yourself in it." But other than the nearby river, there was no water. After some gentle instruction from the lady as to the spring's mysterious location, Bernadette started to claw at some soil and rock, eventually unearthing a previously unknown source of water.

The most remarkable aspect of this true story, though, wouldn't occur until the March 25 apparition. After being prompted by the town priest to ask the vision her name, Bernadette reported something jaw-dropping. The woman had clasped her hands and said in the local dialect, *Que soy era Immaculada Councepciou* ("I am the Immaculate Conception").[1]

Bernadette had no idea what the odd words meant; few people in the world did at the time. Less than four years prior, the Vatican had promulgated the doctrine of the Immaculate Conception. When word spread that the vision affirmed the doctrine in response to Bernadette's name inquiry, skeptics' misgivings about the apparitions were blown to smithereens. They became believers.

Much of the world followed, literally, in step. Presently more than five million people descend annually upon the village at the foothills of the Pyrenees to behold the flowing spring, the niche, and the exact spot where Bernadette knelt to pray with Our Lady. They come, too, in search of healing.

UNCOMMON PEACE

I close my eyes now and see ten thousand pilgrims unified in an interplay of love and light. Holding flickering candles at nightfall, they are like a soft wave of summer fireflies in calm procession. At every Ave Maria—the stirring, universal chant that falls between each decade in the rosary procession—the soft sea of orange flame rises higher into the night sky, to light the esplanade in a blaze of veneration. It seemed each pilgrim was lifting a tiny, iridescent star as a gift to the humble queen who, two thousand years prior, became God's first disciple by obliging his messenger with "May it be done to me according to your word" (Luke 1:38).

Each time thereafter, "Yes." Even at the horror of the cross, "Yes. This plan must be."

I close my eyes and feel the descent of the moonlit switchback that zigzags down into the grotto, the heart of Lourdes. The path is the secret route pilgrims take when the Domain is locked late at night. It is 2 AM, and Krista can't keep away from this rocky outcrop where Our Lady smiled at a girl unaccustomed to such warmth. I am my wife's sleepy escort.

We are descending, and Krista is tearing up because she has begun the unraveling of her own pain in Lourdes—her empty womb, her hell dealing with a husband with blood in his brain, her abandonment of horses. The list runs on; some of the deeper tides of pain I do not even know.

I am the *malade* (the sick one), graciously invited by Michele Bowe, the thoughtful Hospitaller of the Order of Malta's Federal Association. Michele read an article I had written long ago and kept tabs on me over the years. When she heard about my brain issue, she asked a mutual priest friend to invite me to Lourdes as a malade.

But things have been unexpectedly turned upside down here. I've been a wellspring of thanksgiving—giving thanks to God that I'm alive, thanking Krista for her care, thanking those who prayed for me and Italian-born neurosurgeon Dr. Daniele Rigamonti, whose capable hands and mind helped begin to shrink my AVM after an apparently successful Gamma Knife procedure at Johns Hopkins earlier in the year.

Meantime, throughout the week Krista has been slowly handing over heartache after heartache to Mary Immaculate, like a small child who stretches a bleeding finger to her mommy. I think of the opening line of the Memorare: "Remember, O most gracious, Virgin Mary, that never was it known that anyone who fled to thy protection, implored thy help, or sought thy intercession was left unaided."

It is thirty-some degrees (Fahrenheit) this night. The snowcapped Pyrenees are at our backs, and although a chilly breeze whips her, Krista is warm. Earlier this day several thousand pilgrims visited this spot, which is carved into the minds of millions of Christians. Now only four or five people are here.

It is noiseless. It seems all of Lourdes is asleep. Thousands of flamed candles set in nearby stands pop,

pop, pop in the river breeze. The scent of a flower follows us as heavy clouds lie low above the ever-rushing waters of the Gave. We step past the enormous iron candelabrum and into the grotto.

We brush our fingertips over the smooth rock and linger beneath the niche that is replicated all over the world, like Assisi's first crèche. We stand in wonder and awe, half-expecting graces to smash through our heavy jackets and drop us to the stone floor with a surge of love and tenderness. We seem detached from the world, even from ourselves, as a deep peace penetrates us.

Earlier in the week we offered each of the handwritten special prayer intentions from our family and friends. But now we begin the release of our own unwritten petitions. The sensation of handing over our deepest hurts and longings to Our Lady—at the very spot where she once appeared—is difficult to describe. Later Krista told me what she felt that night: "It seemed like she was right there, smiling, knowing everything. It felt like I was being listened to and loved."

I can close my eyes and see Steven Malnight, the kind-hearted auxiliary Order of Malta knight who pulled me one day while I sat uncomfortably in my small blue cart. (All malades are pulled in these carts on pilgrimages.) Steve's around my age. He's a funny, intelligent, and successful vice president of a large company in San Francisco. At breakfast he had asked if he could accompany me to the baths, where many certified miracles have come to pass. "Sure," I said, thinking nothing of it.

So Steve was beside me as we awaited our turn in the baths. A sign near the grotto demanded silence, so we didn't exchange a word for quite some time—which was difficult for us.

Twelve hours later we had French beers with some other guys at the lively St. Sauveur Hotel bar. I poked fun at Steve for accidentally tripping an elderly Carmelite nun earlier in the day. He ripped me for the hundred-plus-pound, rocket ship–sized candle I was asked to carry from my cart the first day of our trip. (No, you will never see these pictures.) Steve and I talked baseball, Notre Dame sports, our jobs, our families.

Then he turned serious.

"You know, Kevin, I want to tell you the reason I asked if I could accompany you to the baths. I wanted to go to the baths to pray specifically for your healing and your intentions," Steve said. "I came to Lourdes hoping to understand what it is to serve others totally and unconditionally. That's what I was trying to do this morning. Today, praying for your healing was the whole purpose of my day."

I bought the next round.

Dangerous Place, Faith

While talking with Steve, I thought about how cool it was to be a Catholic in Lourdes. It's sort of like a Catholic Disneyland. There are long lines to get into daily Mass, torch-lit rosary processions, Eucharistic processions, trips to Bernadette's old house, the Stations of the Cross, and of course, the baths. Later there's the line at the hotel bar with twenty or so new friends. On those cozy nights, when a piano banged in the background and impromptu songs floated about the noisy room, we enjoyed letting our guards down and sharing our faith stories.

But there is a potential danger to Lourdes, just as there is in calling myself a Roman Catholic. With the multitudinous outward signs of grace in both this Pyrenees town and my pilgrim Christian faith, I can easily lose myself and rest easy within the emotion and grandeur of it all. Woolen scapulars, toenail relics, pine-built confessional booths, ascending incense smoke, solemnities, holy cards, tabernacles, monstrances, miracles, martyrs, and multilayered mysteries are merely a pile of pious gobbledygook if I'm a man with the constitution of dust.

What good is Lourdes or any of the aforementioned signs and symbols of my faith if I don't bring it to life in the world? If I don't carry the truth of Jesus and his unbending message of incorruptible love to others, why even bother calling myself a Catholic? What good is it if I'm a pious wimp in a world that aches for substance and meaning?

What good is going to Communion each week if I treat my family poorly? What good is the confessional box if I keep bringing back the same old stuff? What good is a dead soul who sings "Be Not Afraid" really, really loud but has no relationship with Christ?

And what good would Lourdes have been if I had left it all there? As Bernadette herself said near the end of her life, "Lourdes is not heaven."[2] Even in the wake of the astounding occurrences that unfolded before her, Bernadette was wise to the fact that the apparitions would be considered little more than a fairy tale unless she brought heaven's message of love into the world. She understood that unless her encounters with Mary became transformational, her time in the grotto would be just a cheap thrill and a waste of time.

Providentially, though, St. Bernadette was transformed. And many of the three hundred million who've visited Lourdes since then have been changed forever too.

A friendly young man named Marcus Menough, a candidate for the Order of Malta, is one of them. One night he told Krista and me about his visit to Lourdes the previous year. Anger and impatience were the issues he dragged into the grotto late one night with his wife, Angie. There Marcus pleaded his cause to Mary, the advocate. Then, right then, his world changed. He felt every shred of anger being tended to and lifted away by Our Lady. The eyes of his soul were opened as he recited the rosary aloud with Angie. When he smelled the roses that his wife couldn't, he understood that he had been granted Mary's grace and that his anger issues had been plucked from within.

Marcus returned to his home in Houston transformed. Now he prays the rosary daily with his family. He initiated a rosary program, "Children of Our Mother," at nearby archdiocesan schools. Two years later the program is booming. His goal is for every Catholic school in America to have students pray and grasp the power of the rosary— and for teachers and parents to explain how it promotes spiritual growth and internal peace and will inevitably help end abortion.

Marcus was blessed. Mary invited him to be in better alignment with her son, and the Houstonian obliged. "I am an entirely different man now," Marcus said. "Something monumental happened to me that night while praying at the grotto. Mary changed my life."

But even in Mary-mad Lourdes, we know the Virgin— the preeminent model of grace, obedience, and fortitude —is merely a vessel that carries us closer to her carpenter son. That's why she came to the Massabielle cave: She wanted to let Bernadette and the world know that her son loved unreservedly. Tell others to do penance, pray for sinners, and gather together to feel the almighty presence of my son here, Mary encouraged.

Bernadette was permitted a luminous vision. Life and even trips to Lourdes are rarely that miraculous though. Many millions of the sick who have arrived in the small town in southern France with a clearheaded hope of a cure have died without one. Upon their return home their torturous journeys were merely extended, not set right. I imagine a few of the malades on my trip will soon be among the deceased.

Even Bernadette, at the time of her third apparition, was told by Mary, who did not mince words: "I do not promise to make you happy in this life but in the other."[3] Dying with excruciating bone cancer in a convent in Nevers, France, Bernadette rebuffed those who offered to take her back to the healing waters she had unearthed. She knew her earthly role: find Jesus in her suffering and ascend Calvary's hill alongside him, until the pain at last ended.

JESUS IN THE PAIN

One day in Lourdes I was invited to have lunch with Bishop Emeritus William Curlin. This invitation was quite an honor, considering he was not only one of Mother Teresa of Calcutta's best friends for twenty-five years but also her spiritual director. He had just celebrated an informal Mass for two hundred or so people in the basement of our hotel. He gave a memorable homily, encouraging us to tap into the Jesus who lives within each of us. We are Christ's loving hands that reach out to an aching world, he reminded us.

At lunch I told the bishop how his words had touched me. He then related a story about Mother Teresa.

"I remember being in Calcutta with Mother once, and she asked me if I wanted to see Jesus," Bishop Curlin recalled. "So she takes me around the corner of this poor, poor area and stops at a sick man lying on the ground. He has sores all over his body. There are maggots, bugs all around. Then she stoops down and cradles him in her arms with great love and warmth, just as a mother does her baby.

"Then Mother looked up at me and said, 'Here he is.'"

Bishop Curlin has loads of these stories. After meeting Mother Teresa in the slums of Washington, D.C., in the 1970s, he became perhaps the greatest confidant of the Albanian-born "Saint of the Gutters" during the latter part of her forty-year period of darkness. It was a time when she rarely felt the consolation of the very Savior she managed to see in the poor she tirelessly loved. Bishop Curlin was the one who suggested to Mother Teresa that her darkness was perhaps her gift from God.

No one, of course, knowingly chooses to suffer. Mother Teresa, I imagine, hungered to feel the touch of Christ to help propel her into the countless rotting villages she visited. Her cross was bringing Christ's love to the dying without ever really feeling his presence herself. But she never walked away.

In her moments of greatest vulnerability and hopelessness, she intuitively knew what Christ desired from her: a patient acceptance of her darkness. So she walked boldly forward, finding Christ in the leper even when she couldn't find him within herself. She felt alone in her love. And when she felt that, she understood what it was to be Jesus on the cross. Mother Teresa, a living, breathing, pulsating psalm of lamentation, was wide awake to her bitter reality: Sure, Jesus was standing beside her, but he was wordless within her pit.

While Bishop Curlin was telling stories about his old friend and the future saint, I was thinking of the dozens of malades at the surrounding dining room tables. Earlier that morning the bishop had blessed each of us with Lourdes water in a disarming ritual that brought many tears. One by one the sick and dying had approached him in a surrendering juxtaposition of suffering and hope—just like the band of Gospel characters who reached out for the Nazarene: the roadside leper, the paralytic lowered from the rooftop, Bartimaeus, the hemorrhaging woman, the blind beggar, Peter's mother-in-law, perhaps even that earless soldier in Gethsemane at the end. For each of us it was a bittersweet procession of faith and surrender to God's puzzling plan of pain in our lives.

As onlookers marveled, the sick came forward with their own personal insights into the mystery of their pain. Mine was the awareness that God had permitted certain pains and powerlessness in order to draw me closer to him. He's dropped anvils, I believe, as invitations for me to live and love as he did. It's communion with me that he wants.

As I received my special blessing, two hundred or so pilgrims recited the rosary aloud, requesting the intercession of Mary on my behalf. For the pilgrims it was a chance to give of themselves yet again. They knew the long line of malades was an interconnected "one" in its suffering. They knew that the mystery of pain remained a bitter cross and blurred wilderness for some and that they couldn't help us much in that regard. So they prayed the rosary, and their care for us was as palpable as Mary's love was for Bernadette in the grotto.

In Massabielle Christ's Mother entered into the darkness. In corrugated Calcutta huts and on thousands of no-name streets, a future saint did. When I was in Lourdes, individuals like Steve and Marcus chose to love the sick and dying from sunup to sundown. For a short while they were the daylight in the malades' mysterious darkness. For a short while they were Jesus Christ reaching out in the mess.

This disarming symmetry wasn't lost on Spanish mystic St. Teresa of Avila: "You are Christ's hands. Christ has no body now on earth but yours, no hands but yours, no feet but yours. Yours are the eyes through which Christ's compassion looks out on the world; yours are the feet with which he is to go about doing good; yours are the hands with which he is to bless men now."[4]

I was on silent retreat recently when I met a fellow retreatant suffering from paranoia and hallucinations, among other things. His delusions were made clear one evening when I went to the small upstairs chapel to pray before sleep. From nowhere he rushed up to me in tabernacle candlelight to exclaim forcefully, "And who are you?"

Since up until then it had been a day of total silence, his outburst felt like a Blitzkrieg.

He looked like a cattle farmer and wore enormous, tan clodhoppers that clomped, clomped, clomped past my (locked) door at odd hours of the night. Most places he went, he whispered to himself and tugged on his large St. Benedict medal. I prayed for him the night he almost scared the intestines out of me, then asked God to make me a vehicle of love to him the following day.

Well, over the next four days, this suffering man became a friend. We took walks together, had late-night talks in the dining room, shared Scripture passages and reading material, and generally got along well.

It was easy to see the immensity of this man's interior suffering. In his moments of clarity, a soft glow of peace shone on his face. He explained in detail the ever-present hallucinations. He suspected, for the first few days of the retreat, that I was a CIA agent tracking him. He knew it was outlandish to imagine such a thing, but he couldn't restrain the suspicions that bore into his mind.

"I don't know how to help end your paranoia, but maybe you should try something," I said. "Whenever you feel like the paranoia is starting to overwhelm you, fold your hands and say a Hail Mary. Maybe the prayer won't penetrate the paranoia. And maybe you won't be able to finish the prayer. But Our Mother and Jesus will know you're reaching out for them in your distress. They'll be right beside you in your pain."

I gave him some Scripture passages that I thought would be helpful. He seemed grateful.

It's God, of course, who writes these moments into our lives. Within the details of our lives, he is everywhere. There's deep mystery to my faith, but I don't think this is part of it. I think when we choose to embrace these occasions of small sacrifice with love, we become fleeting physical manifestations of Christ.

Many of the pages you've read detail periods of my pain and of Christ working within it. Nothing about my story of suffering is so unique; it's one of many.

But I use this particular story of my encounter with this man on retreat for some cushion to step atop my microscopic soapbox and propose what I believe to be our most abundant and meaningful affliction: the unremitting pinpricks we encounter from the moment we wake to the moment our eyelids finally drop at night. All the grand intentions I had entering the silent retreat were whitewashed by my ongoing meetings with this kind, tortured gentleman. I had only wanted to disappear by myself beneath the turquoise sky to spend time in prayer. But even a second or two spent on "WWJD discernment" told me another path to take: Welcome this man into your life whenever his clomping boots come your way.

It seems to me that these miniature bothers in our lives are indications of God's fullest measure of love for us, because they are his very invitations to attempt to reflect him. These daily moments of sacrifice are sacred because by obliging them, we are enabled to become the very people he intends. Obliging these moments leads to a kind of modern-day martyrdom; we die to ourselves some when seeing them through.

There are no fairies floating about sprinkling love dust on the lonely, suffering, and confused. As Tommy would say in his no-nonsense way, "Just get out there and be Christ to them." He knew that faith without action is little more than a hollow boast. That's why he was a flash of light in this world.

These thorns are our gateways to God. And these thorns matter.

It's by deflecting our natures and entering into these momentary drudgeries with a surrendering heart that we better understand what it is to love like Christ. And awesomely, it's often in the very moments of these small deserts that his graces spring up within us—the graces that inch us ever closer to reflecting his immeasurable love.

"Dad, can you watch me ride my bike around the cul-de-sac (350 times in a row)? And then can we play Monopoly when we go inside?"

"Sump pump broke. Have you seen the basement?"

"Honey, I know you just got home from work, but can you drive Gabby out to Edgewater for Irish step dancing?"

If we can't find a way to handle these pedestrian bothers, well, we're certainly going to suffer when our life suddenly capsizes and we're sent to our knees.

James began his letter: "Consider it all joy, my brothers, when you encounter various trials, for you know that the testing of your faith produces perseverance" (James 1:2–3). Those early disciples had to work through the chance that they just might get their heads cut off. I need to work through giving Sean a ride to a birthday party across town.

I haven't a clue how my day of judgment will unfold, but I have a suspicion that God's not going to be speaking much. I do think he'll ask one thing of me though: "But, Kevin, how did you love?"

As an ex-reporter, that's my hunch anyhow.

CHAPTER ONE: FEROCIOUS LOVE

1. Thérèse of Lisieux, *Thoughts of Saint Thérèse* (Charlotte, N.C.: Tan, 1988), p. 133.

2. Faustina Kowalska, *Divine Mercy in My Soul* (Marian, 1987), no. 57, as quoted in George Kosicki, *Revelations of Divine Mercy: Daily Readings from the Diary of Blessed Faustina Kowalska* (Ann Arbor, Mich.: Servant, 1996), p. 55.

3. John Paul II, *Salvifici Doloris,* Apostolic Letter on the Christian Meaning of Human Suffering, 12, February 11, 1984, www.vatican.va.

CHAPTER SIX: FORWARD AT A CRAWL

1. Manuel Perez-Rivas, "Evidence Outlined in Slaying of Priest," *The Washington Post,* June 20, 2000.

2. Reported by Pat Collins on NBC television affiliate WRC, Washington, D.C., June 21, 2000.

CHAPTER SEVEN: SATAN'S FLIGHT

1. Susan Levine, "Priest's Killer Tells Court of Struggle; Lucas Admits Altering His Account," *The Washington Post,* May 31, 2001.

2. Levine.

CHAPTER TEN: VACATION REALIZATIONS

1. Jonathan Morris, "A Different Kind of Miracle on the Hudson," *The Wall Street Journal*, August 16, 2009, http://online.wsj.com.

CHAPTER ELEVEN: NIGHT OF LIGHTS

1. Willa Cather, *Death Comes for the Archbishop* (New York: Vintage, 1990), p. 50.

CHAPTER TWELVE: LOURDES

1. As quoted in Pope John Paul II, Homily at Lourdes, France, on the Occasion of the 150th Anniversary of the Promulgation of the Dogma of the Immaculate Conception, August 15, 2004, www.vatican.va.

2. Bernadette Soubirous, as quoted at Lourdes-france.org.

3. Quoted in "Diary of the Apparitions," *Lourdes Magazine*, June/July 2005, p. 26.

4. Teresa of Avila, as quoted at www.thecatholicspirit.com.